Black Battles with Dogs, Return to the Desert, Roberto Zucco

Koltès's plays have been phenomenally successful, not just in Europe but worldwide. They present a vision of the harsh realities of late twentieth-century life, influenced by Genet and Fugard, combined with a formal approach to dramatic dialogue in the French classical tradition.

Black Battles with Dogs: 'Koltès's view of men is ugly and comfortless: reconciliation is impossible; bonds are formed in extremity and broken with violence ... a compulsive piece of theatre.' *Observer*

Return to the Desert: 'It has, above all, what makes Bernard-Marie Koltès a first-class dramatist: the ideas, in perpetually inventive motion, are supported by language, and language by ideas. This seems to spring naturally, and there is nothing more rare. This thrust, which gives light and force and irradiates with splendour everything written by Koltès, is quite exceptional.' *Le Monde*

'*Roberto Zucco*, the play about an Italian serial killer, has become a French classic.' *Independent on Sunday*

Bernard-Marie Koltès was 'a creator of a mythology of the underworld, a champion of the underdog and the lone wolf, and a pioneer of a wholly new style of dramatic writing.' *The Times*

The volume is introduced by David Bradby, Professor of Drama at Royal Holloway, University of London.

Bernard-Marie Koltès was born in Metz in 1948. He studied at the School attached to the Théâtre National de Strasbourg, where he began to write plays. His dramatic monologue *La Nuit juste avant les forêts* was premièred at the Avignon Festival in 1977 and staged as *Twilight Zone* by Pierre Audi in Edinburgh and London in 1981. His career was closely linked with that of Patrice Chéreau, who produced all his major plays: *Combat de nègre et de chiens* (Théâtre des Amandiers, Paris, 1983; première New York, 1982; Gate Theatre, London, 1988); *Quai ouest* (Théâtre des Amandiers, Paris, 1986); *Dans la solitude des champs de coton* (Théâtre des Amandiers, Paris, 1987; Edinburgh Festival, 1995); *Le Retour au désert* (Théâtre du Rond-Point, Paris, 1988). His final play, *Roberto Zucco*, was premièred at the Schaubühne, Berlin, in 1990. He died of Aids in 1989.

Methuen World Classics *and*
Methuen Contemporary Dramatists *include*

BERNARD-MARIE KOLTÈS

Plays: 1

Black Battles with Dogs
translated by David Bradby and Maria M. Delgado

Return to the Desert
translated by David Bradby

Roberto Zucco
translated by Martin Crimp

edited and introduced by David Bradby

Methuen Drama

METHUEN CONTEMPORARY DRAMATISTS

This collection first published in Great Britain 1997
by Methuen Drama
an imprint of Reed International Books Ltd
Michelin House, 81 Fulham Road, London SW3 6RB
and Auckland, Melbourne, Singapore and Toronto

ISBN 0-413-70240-5

A CIP catalogue record for this book
is available from the British Library

Typeset by Wilmaset Ltd, Birkenhead, Wirral
Printed and bound in Great Britain by Cox & Wyman Ltd, Reading

Contents

Bernard-Marie Koltès:
Chronology

1948   Birth of Bernard-Marie Koltès (9 April) at Metz, a town in the eastern part of France. His father, a professional soldier, was away in Algeria for much of the 1950s.

1958–62   Koltès's secondary schooling began against a background of bombings and disturbances as the crisis of the Algerian conflict pushed France to the brink of civil war.

1967   After completing school in Metz, Koltès went to Strasbourg, where he attended courses at the School of Journalism. He also studied music, and even considered becoming a professional organist.

1968   In January he saw Maria Casarès, at Strasbourg, playing the central role in Seneca's *Medea*; this was his first visit to a theatre and had a profound effect on him. During the May 1968 occupations of colleges and factories Koltès avoided political involvement. In the summer he travelled to Paris, and then to New York.

1969   First attempt at writing for the theatre: a stage adaptation of Gorky's *My Childhood*, entitled *Les Amertumes* (*Bitternesses*); he sent the play to Hubert Gignoux, director of the Strasbourg National Drama School, asking for advice.

1970   Koltès directed a few friends in a production of his play at the Théâtre du Quai, Strasbourg (performances in May and June). Hubert Gignoux saw the production and invited Koltès to join his course in the *régie* (technical) section of the School. He joined, but dropped out during his second year.

1971   He wrote and directed his second and third plays in the same little student Théâtre du Quai: *La Marche* (*The March*), based on the Song of Songs, and *Procès ivre* (*Drunken Trial*), based on Dostoevsky's *Crime and Punishment*.

1972   *L'Héritage* (*The Inheritance*) broadcast on local Radio Alsace and then again on France-Culture (produced by Lucien Attoun) with Maria Casarès.

1973   *Récits morts* (*Dead Stories*) directed by Koltès at the Théâtre du Quai. During the 1970s Koltès earned little or nothing from his writing and took casual jobs (e.g. selling tickets in Strasbourg cinemas).

1974   A second play broadcast, first on Radio Alsace and afterwards on France-Culture: *Des Voix sourdes* (*Deaf/Muffled Voices*).

1975–6   Koltès moved to Paris and wrote his first novel, *La Fuite à cheval très loin dans la ville* (*The Flight on Horseback Far Into the Town*) (dated September 1976). The typescript circulated among friends for some years before being published by Les Editions de Minuit in 1984.

1977   Wrote a dramatic monologue, *La Nuit juste avant les forêts* (*The Night Just Before the Forests*), for actor Yves Ferry (whom he had known at the Strasbourg Drama School) and directed him in a performance given on the fringe of the Avignon Theatre Festival. Invited by Bruno Boeglin to observe a series of actors' workshops based on the stories of J. D. Salinger and to write a play inspired by them, he wrote *Sallinger* (sic), directed by Boeglin and performed during the 1977/8 season at his El Dorado theatre in Lyons.

1978   Journey to West Africa, where he visited friends working on a construction site in Nigeria.

1979   Returned to West Africa, visiting Mali and Ivory Coast; six-month trip to Nicaragua (just before the Sandanista revolution) and to Guatemala, during which he wrote *Combat de nègre et de chiens* (*Black Battles with Dogs*). The play was published as a 'tapuscrit' by Théâtre Ouvert – i.e. a limited number of typescripts which are made for circulation among theatre professionals so as to encourage the dissemination of new theatre writing.

1980   Radio broadcast on France-Culture of *Combat de nègre et de chiens*. The text received its first commercial publication in the 'Théâtre Ouvert' series of Stock (Paris) together with *La Nuit juste avant les forêts*.

1981   Four-month visit to New York. Koltès beginning to be known in theatre circles: *La Nuit juste avant les forêts* revived at the Petit Odéon with the actor Richard Fontana. Received a commission for a play by the Comédie Française. Plans made with Françoise Kourilsky for a production of *Combat de nègre et de chiens* in New York.

1982   Returned to New York for world première of *Combat de nègre et de chiens* at Theatre La Mama: the American translation, by Matthew Ward, was originally entitled *Come Dog, Come Night*. At Koltès's insistence, it was later changed to *Struggle of the Dogs and the Black* and published under this title, first in the collection of the New York Ubu Repertory Theatre (1982) and later by Methuen in *New*

French Plays (1989). Koltès translated Athol Fugard's *The Blood Knot* for production at the Avignon Festival.

1983   Patrice Chéreau opened his new Théâtre des Amandiers at Nanterre (on the outskirts of Paris) with the French première of *Combat de nègre et de chiens*. The set (by Richard Peduzzi) was monumental and the cast star-studded: Michel Piccoli, Philippe Léotard, Myriam Boyer, Sidiki Bakaba; the critics were mostly enthusiastic: until his death at the end of the decade, Koltès was widely accepted as the most important new voice in French theatre. From this point on he was able to live from his writing, though he earned more from foreign (especially German) productions than from the exploitation of his work in France. Worked briefly as 'dramaturge' with François Regnault on Chéreau's production of *Les Paravents* (*The Screens*) by Jean Genet; together they published *La Famille des Orties* (*The Nettle Family*).

1984   Journey to Senegal. Publication of *La Nuit juste avant les forêts* (see 1977). Four different productions of *Combat de nègre et de chiens* in German theatres (Frankfurt, Tübingen, Wuppertal and Munich).

1985   Publication of *Quai ouest* by Minuit; world première of the play given in Dutch at the Publiekstheater, Amsterdam.

1986   French première of *Quai ouest*, directed by Patrice Chéreau, with Maria Casarès in the cast, at the Théâtre des Amandiers. The critics were again impressed by the writing, but blamed Chéreau and Peduzzi for crushing the play beneath a monumental production. Koltès responded to a commission by the Avignon Festival for a play in a series with the title 'Oser aimer' ('To dare to love') with a short play, *Tabataba*, about someone who 'dares to love' his motorcycle. Publication of *Dans la solitude des champs de coton* (*In the Solitude of the Cotton Fields*) by Minuit.

1987   First production of *Dans la solitude des champs de coton* by Patrice Chéreau at Nanterre. The role of the Client was taken by Laurent Malet and that of the Dealer by Isaach de Bankolé. In subsequent seasons Chéreau revived this production, taking the role of the Dealer himself; this provoked a temporary break with Koltès, who insisted that he had written the role of the Dealer for a black actor.

1988   Two major firsts for Koltès: *Le Retour au désert* (*Return to the Desert*) received its première in a production by Patrice Chéreau at the Théâtre du Rond-Point in the centre of Paris. Jacqueline Maillan, a popular comic actress for whom he had written it, was in the central role and Michel Piccoli played her brother. At the Théâtre des Amandiers his translation of *A Winter's Tale* was directed by Luc Bondy. In the metro, Koltès was struck by police 'wanted' posters with photos of the murderer Roberto Succo and became interested in his case, especially after he had seen television pictures of Succo's last hours on the roof-top of an Italian prison.

1989   Death of Koltès in Paris a week after his forty-first birthday (15 April). Shortly before his death, he had completed his final play, *Roberto Zucco*.

1990   World première of *Roberto Zucco*, directed by Peter Stein at the Berlin Schaubühne.

Chronology of plays – premières/publications
(from a list by Serge Saada published in *Alternatives Théâtrales*, 35–36, June 1990)

Les Amertumes, adapted from Gorky's novel *Childhood*, produced by the author, Strasbourg, 1970.

La Marche, inspired by the Song of Songs, produced by the author, Strasbourg, 1971.

Procès ivre, inspired by Dostoevsky's novel *Crime and Punishment*, produced by the author, Strasbourg, 1971.

L'Héritage produced on Radio-France Alsace and then again on France-Culture (also radio), 1972.

Récits morts produced by the author, Strasbourg, 1973.

Des Voix sourdes produced on Radio-France Alsace and on France-Culture, 1974.

Le Jour des meurtres dans l'histoire d'Hamlet, 1974.

Sallinger, inspired by the stories of J. D. Salinger, produced by Bruno Boeglin, Lyons, 1977. Published by Minuit, 1995.

La Nuit juste avant les forêts, monologue, produced by the author, Avignon Festival, 1977. Published by Stock/ Théâtre Ouvert, 1980; Minuit, 1988. First English production as *Twilight Zone*, directed by Pierre Audi, Edinburgh Festival and Almeida Theatre, 1981.

Combat de nègre et de chiens published by Stock/Théâtre Ouvert, 1980; Minuit, 1989. First produced by Françoise Kourilsky, La Mama Theatre, New York, 1982, in a translation by Matthew Ward; first French production by Patrice Chéreau, Théâtre des Amandiers, Nanterre, 1983. First English production as *Struggle of the Black Man and the Dogs*, directed by Michael Batz, Gate Theatre, 1988. English publication: *Struggle of the Dogs and the Black* (trans. Matthew Ward) in *New French Plays*, Methuen, 1989.

Le Lien du sang, translation of *The Blood Knot* by Athol Fugard, first produced by Yutaka Wada, Avignon Festival, 1982.

Quai ouest published by Minuit, 1985. First produced by Stephane Stroux in a Dutch translation, Amsterdam, 1985; first French production by Patrice Chéreau, Théâtre des Amandiers, 1986.

Tabataba produced by Hammou Graia, Avignon Festival, 1986. Published by Minuit with *Roberto Zucco* (see below).

Dans la solitude des champs de coton published by Minuit, 1986. First produced by Patrice Chéreau, Théâtre des Amandiers, 1987.

Le Conte d'hiver, translation of *A Winter's Tale* by Shakespeare, first produced by Luc Bondy, Théâtre des Amandiers, 1988. Published by Minuit, 1988.

Le Retour au désert first produced by Patrice Chéreau, Théâtre du Rond-Point, Paris, 1988. Published by Minuit, 1988.

Roberto Zucco first produced by Peter Stein in a German translation by Simon Werle, Schaubühne, Berlin, 1990; first French production by Bruno Boeglin, Théâtre National Populaire, Villeurbanne, 1991. Published by Minuit, with *Tabataba*, 1990.

Introduction

> I have always rather detested theatre because theatre is
> the opposite of life; but I always come back to it and I
> love it because it is the one place where you say: this is
> not life.[1]

Bernard-Marie Koltès, the author of these words, was not
afraid of contradictions. Although a major modern
playwright, he seldom went to the theatre but was a
film fanatic. A compulsive traveller, whose first major
play was set in Africa, he nevertheless insisted that his
sole subject was France. Like Genet, he captured the
argot of the Arab immigrant or of the French criminal
underclass, and yet the formality of his language recalls
the classical purity of Racine. His status as an icon of high
postmodernist art – hailed by Heiner Müller[2] and
produced by Peter Stein and Patrice Chéreau – might
suggest a forbidding avant-garde writer, yet his plays tell
absorbing stories, arouse laughter in the theatre, and his
own tastes were for performance that is popular and
accessible. His heroes were the Kung-Fu star Bruce Lee
and the Jamaican reggae singer Bob Marley. He disliked
any kind of theorising, and when he spoke about writing,
he concentrated on the craft of the playwright rather than
on dramatic theories or ideas.

Like Chekhov before him, Koltès was convinced that
the plays he wrote were comic, and wanted them to be

[1] 'Un Hangar à l'ouest' in *Roberto Zucco*, Paris: Minuit, 1990, p. 120.
(This article was written at the time of the French production of *Quai
ouest*: 1986.)

[2] See the interview with Heiner Müller in *Alternatives Théâtrales*, 35/6,
June 1990, pp. 12–15. Müller translated *Quai ouest* into German in 1986.

performed lightly and rapidly. He once said that his ideal actors would speak his lines like a child reciting a lesson while suffering from an urgent need to pee.[3] Yet the subjects dealt with in his plays are anything but light. They are subjects of general concern to Europeans living in the last decades of the twentieth century: the conditions of urban life; the disparities between rich and poor, natives and immigrants; the blurring of cultural boundaries and cultural identities; relationships between first and third worlds and the global dimension of large commercial organisations that bind us all together, whether we like it or not; racism, crime, violence; fears of things falling apart set against myths of utopian wholeness. He presented these subjects with a rawness and urgency rarely matched in the theatre today.

Koltès never aligned himself with a given political position, but all his plays deal with ideology. The private relationships between his characters can never be separated from their social and political interactions. He wrote that:

> I have never liked love stories. They tell you so little. I don't believe in the love relationship ... If you want to tell a story with any subtlety you have to take a different route. For me the 'deal' is a sublime means. It really encompasses everything else. It would be good to write a play between a man and a woman where everything is about 'business'.[4]

Koltès succeeded in writing the kind of play he alludes to here. It is the second in this volume, *Return to the Desert*. In this drama every aspect of the relationship between Mathilde and Adrien is revealed as rooted in a business transaction of some kind, even those aspects of family life that they consider to be the most private are subject to never-ending negotiations.

[3] 'Pour mettre en scène *Quai ouest*', in *Quai ouest*, Minuit, 1985, p.104.

[4] Quoted by Michel Bataillon in 'Koltès, le flâneur infatigable', *Théâtre en Europe*, 18, September 1988, p. 26.

In line with this vision, Koltès saw human relations as a series of *deals* (he always used the English/American word and did not try to translate it). He explained what he meant by the term in the epigraph he wrote for a major play not included in this volume, *In the Solitude of the Cotton Fields*:

> A *deal* is a commercial transaction concerning values that are banned or subject to strict controls, and which is conducted in neutral spaces, indeterminate and not intended for this purpose, between suppliers and consumers, by means of tacit agreement, conventional signs, or conversations with double meanings – whose aim is to circumvent the risks of betrayal or swindle implicit in this kind of operation – at any time of day or night, with no reference to the regulation opening hours for officially registered trading establishments, but usually at times when the latter are closed.

This explanation of the term, written in a parody of bureaucratic or contractual language, suggests a very Balzacian view of society, peopled by individuals all governed by the feverish need to buy and sell. In addition, it expresses this in terms that are deeply coloured by our late twentieth-century awareness of commerce as a global activity with a secretive or underhand life of its own, beyond any official controls.

Koltès's description of the *deal* goes further, suggesting that theatre itself is a form of transactional communication. For if Koltès's view of society bears comparison with Balzac's human comedy, his literary method is closer to the disciplined focus on moments of great intensity that we associate with Racine. Koltès's comment on the *deal* neatly identifies the fundamental nature of any dramatic dialogue or theatrical situation: a tension arising from an encounter between two people, each of whom wants something from the other, each of whom is using words transactionally, i.e. is seeking to do something to the other by means of the words that are spoken.

All of Koltès's characters use words in this way and all

find themselves embroiled in conflicts. Each of the three plays that follow presents a contest of an intensely dramatic kind. The first play (with the key word *'combat'*, i.e. battle, in its title) presents a situation of multi-layered conflict: the battles take place not only between individuals, but also between societies, cultures, ideologies. *Return to the Desert* enacts a conflict that is to do with ownership: Adrien and Mathilde (brother and sister) fight about who can lay claim to the family property in a manner reminiscent of Mauriac, but their struggle also suggests a deeper and wider conflict about which social class will inherit France. In the last play, the main conflict pits the outlaw, Roberto Zucco, against the whole of law-abiding society; but the play also depicts violence within the family unit, evoking the conflictual nature of relationships between parents and children, brothers and sisters. In short, the situations in Koltès's plays are always dynamic, rooted in conflicts, negotiations, betrayals, mutilations and murder.

The playwright: Bernard-Marie Koltès 1948–89

Koltès's life, on the surface at least, contained none of the deadly struggles that characterise his plays. He was not one to man the barricades or put out slogans, even during his student days in the late 1960s. In fact he tended to avoid conflict whenever possible; though homosexual, he never 'came out' or aligned himself with gay liberation movements, and the fact that he was suffering from Aids was a closely guarded secret for most of the 1980s. This was not from lack of courage on his part, but rather from a kind of natural reserve: he had no desire to serve as a rallying cry or to get caught up in fashionable causes. In this, as in many other ways, he resembled Genet, who campaigned in favour of the Black Panthers and the Palestine Liberation Organisation, but who kept his distance from political or social struggles in France (unlike Sartre who frequently involved himself in the campaigns of the day).

Koltès was born and brought up in Metz, an industrial

and military town in the eastern part of France, where his father was a professional soldier. He had two brothers, Jean-Marie was the eldest, then came François and, one year younger, Bernard-Marie. His grandparents on both sides of the family were local people, miners and foresters, and family memories stretched back to the time when Alsace/Lorraine had been annexed by the Germans. His mother was a fervent Catholic: her sons were given Catholic names and were sent, not to the state school, but to the Catholic college in the centre of Metz.

For most of the 1950s, the father was absent in Algeria, so his children saw little of him, but their teachers would have left them in no doubt that the struggle in Algeria had a crusading side to it, representing the struggle of enlightened Christian France against the dark forces of Islam. This was the last and bitterest of France's colonial wars. In the eyes of the vast majority of the French population, Algeria was not a separate country at all, but part of France that happened to be situated on the other side of the Mediterranean sea. The struggle against the FLN (Algerian National Liberation Front) was seen as a fight to preserve the integrity of the nation in much the same way as the fight against the IRA in Northern Ireland has seemed, to some British people, to be about pre- serving the United Kingdom. It was a colonial conflict which would later have a central place in Koltès's plays.

At the end of the 1950s a group of army generals staged a coup against the French government. It was a last-ditch attempt to prevent Algeria being granted independence. They were out-manoeuvred by the superior political skill of de Gaulle, who had recently become president and had inaugurated the Fifth Republic. In 1960 General Massu, one of the ring-leaders, was recalled to Metz where he was given the post of military governor to keep him occupied. Koltès recalled his mixture of fear and fascination as he watched Massu's paratroopers march- ing through the streets.[5] In the two years that remained

[5] From an interview published in *Le Républicain Lorrain*, 27 October 1988, and quoted in *Alternatives Théâtrales*, 35/6, June 1990, p.125.

until the peace agreements of Evian brought the conflict to an end there was constant tension in Metz, which sometimes erupted into pitched street-battles between 'paras' and Arabs. One night there was a major disorder that left seventeen Arabs dead. In order to try to contain the situation the Prefect decreed a no-go area for French people in the part of town where most of the Arabs lived, thus effectively creating a ghetto. This had a considerable effect on the lives of the young Koltès brothers, since the school they attended was situated in the no-go area. The territoriality that was to be so important a part of Koltès's plays can be traced back to these early experiences.

After secondary school, Bernard-Marie went on to study at the School of Journalism in Strasbourg. He was already an accomplished pianist and continued to take lessons after the move to Strasbourg. One teacher who particularly influenced him was an expert in the music of Messian, and for a while Koltès planned a career as a professional organist. But everything changed for him in 1968. This was the year in which a near-revolution swept through France and universities, up and down the country, were occupied by students. The Strasbourg faculty hall had a particularly fine grand piano, and throughout May 1968 François Koltès remembers his brother seated at this piano filling the hall with the music of Bach, Liszt and Messian. But the real change in the future playwright's life came when he discovered for the first time the pleasures of travel, going first to Paris and then, in the same year, to New York city. For the twenty-year-old boy, brought up in a protective Catholic family and used to life in the French provinces, the discovery of New York, especially of its black population, affected him deeply. He developed a passion for black music, idolising the blues singers Billie Holiday and Otis Redding, and returned frequently to New York, which became the setting for one of his major plays (*Quai ouest*).

On his return to France he began to write plays and quickly abandoned the study of classical music. Throughout the 1970s he lived from hand to mouth taking all kinds of temporary jobs to pay the rent. His favourite was taking tickets at the cinema, because this allowed him freedom to indulge his passion for films. He said later that no matter how bad the film he always found something interesting in cinema, whereas most of the time he found theatre unbearable. It was a time when it was relatively rare to see the work of new French playwrights performed, and top directors (men such as Planchon, Vitez or Chéreau) preferred to present lavish reinterpretations of the classics. Inspired by his first visit to the theatre, when he had seen Maria Casarès playing the title role in Seneca's *Medea*, Koltès's early plays were intensely theatrical; they were all adaptations because he saw them as apprentice pieces through which he was learning his craft. His appetite for reading, especially the Russian classics, emerges in the models he chose to adapt for his early plays – Gorky's *My Childhood* and Dostoevsky's *Crime and Punishment* were both among them.

Within four years he had written six plays, four of which he staged with a group of friends in a student theatre in Strasbourg, and two of which were broadcast on both local and national radio (the first with Maria Casarès in the title role). He also attracted the attention of Hubert Gignoux, who was at this time head of the National Drama School situated in Strasbourg. Gignoux attended the production of Koltès's first play and, on the strength of this, invited him to join the School, in the technical department. Koltès did so, and maintained a friendly relationship with Gignoux for the rest of his life, although he dropped out of the course, preferring to devote his mental energies to writing and staging his own plays. He would always show drafts of his plays to Gignoux, and Gignoux was responsible for bringing him to the attention of others working in the theatre, notably Lucien Attoun, director of 'Théâtre Ouvert', and most importantly Patrice Chéreau, who directed all but one of Koltès's major plays in the 1980s.

Lucien Attoun, who, with his wife Micheline, directs 'Théâtre Ouvert', is a broadcaster, publisher and entrepreneur of experimental theatre. He produced the first two national radio broadcasts of plays by Koltès (see Chronology) and published his first dramatic monologue, *The Night Just Before the Forests*, together with *Black Battles with Dogs*, in 1980. For most of the 1970s, however, Koltès found it hard to establish himself as a professional playwright. His response was a characteristic one: he decided to move away from Strasbourg, leaving behind his network of theatre contacts there and attempting a different kind of writing. He moved into a flat in Paris and wrote a novel (untranslated as yet), *La Fuite à cheval très loin dans la ville* (*The Flight on Horseback Far Into the Town*).

But in 1977 he was seduced back to theatre work. In this year he met Bruno Boeglin, a theatre director who had a group of actors developing improvisations on themes taken from the writings of the American writer J. D. Salinger. Boeglin shared his passion for travel and, especially, his growing interest in South America, which both men were to visit in the following years. Koltès spent some time watching Boeglin's company at work and then, drawing on their improvisations, wrote *Sallinger* (sic), which was performed by Boeglin's company in Lyons during the following season. At the request of Yves Ferry, an actor whom Koltès had known since they were both at the Strasbourg drama school, he also wrote a dramatic monologue, which he regarded as his first truly original play. This was *La Nuit juste avant les forêts* (*The Night Just Before the Forests* – originally *The Night Just Before the Forests of Nicaragua*). Koltès directed Ferry in its first performance at the Avignon Festival of 1977. The play was well received by the critics and this experience, together with his participation in the work of Bruno Boeglin's company, gave him renewed belief in his powers as a playwright.

During the next two years he travelled extensively in Africa and South America, becoming especially interested

in the civil war in Nicaragua. His sympathy for people
suffering from oppression was evident, but he still
remained clear of direct political involvement. Two
stories that he wrote in Nicaragua in 1978 were
published after his death.[6] These stories reveal his
ability to create a compelling stream-of-consciousness
prose style, evoking the mentalities of people caught up in
a struggle for survival in places where armed squads roam
the night, but where even the most destitute people have
their heads filled with dreams of fabulous wealth in
America. These stories are reminiscent of the travel
writer and novelist Bruce Chatwin and his ability to bring
places alive through the eyes of a traveller. Koltès had the
idea for *Black Battles with Dogs* when staying in a camp
for expatriates working on an engineering project in
Nigeria: the cries of the night-watchmen guarding the
camp provided his first inspiration. The play was later
written in the course of a six-month stay in Guatemala.

About this time he also saw Patrice Chéreau's production of *La Dispute* by Marivaux. He was impressed by
Chéreau's austere staging and by his revelation of a cruel
modernity in the dialogue of the eighteenth-century
playwright, and he set his sights on getting his own
plays produced by Chéreau. This meant that *Black
Battles with Dogs* had to wait three years for its first
French production, since Chéreau was at this time
negotiating his move from the Théâtre National Populaire in Villeurbanne (where he had been co-artistic
director with Roger Planchon throughout the 1970s) to
his own theatre, the Théâtre des Amandiers, in the
northern industrial suburbs of Paris at Nanterre. In the
meantime, Koltès travelled back and forth between Paris
and New York, where Françoise Kourilsky produced the
world première of the play (in English translation) at the
experimental theatre La Mama in 1982.

The 1980s were for Bernard-Marie Koltès a time of

---

[6] Entitled simply *Deux Nouvelles*, and included in *Prologue*, Minuit,
1991.

both fulfilment and frustration. On the one hand he developed a close working relationship with Patrice Chéreau, who committed himself to producing every new work that Koltès wrote. On the other hand Koltès was upset to find that his plays were produced more abroad than in France (his financial independence during the last years of his life was largely due to royalties from the German theatres) and that these foreign productions often seemed wilfully to flout his intentions. Chéreau's production of *Black Battles with Dogs* was a huge critical success in France but did not give rise to other productions of the play. This neglect would continue until his death. It seemed that other directors were too much in awe of Chéreau and did not wish to risk unflattering comparisons with new stagings of their own.

Nevertheless, the unequivocal support of a major director such as Chéreau was certainly a factor in Koltès's growing confidence and increased output during this period. Equally important to him was being part of a professional producing company for which he did other, occasional work. For example, in 1983 he had a brief spell working on Chéreau's production of Genet's play *The Screens* and in 1987 he made a translation of Shakespeare's *Winter's Tale*, which was directed at the Théâtre des Amandiers by Luc Bondy. He said, in an interview, that he had enjoyed this greatly and would like to translate another, perhaps *Richard III* or *King Lear*. Towards the end of his life, he appeared to be moving away from the rather neo-classical respect for the three unities that characterised his early plays and towards a much greater freedom in the use of dramatic form, a freedom he said he had learned from Shakespeare. His new-found freedom is visible for the first time in *Return to the Desert*, written in 1988.

From 1975 until his death Koltès had a flat in Paris. He never felt the need to identify with a particular community, valuing the freedom to travel above everything. He wrote that he lacked all feeling for 'home' but experienced something of the comfort and security

normally associated with home when he listened to Bob
Marley. One of his favourite Marley songs, 'Running
Away', sums up the restlessness and desire for escape that
were a central part of Koltès's spiritual make-up. In the
last year of his life his freedom of movement was severely
curtailed by his physical condition. He compensated for
this by writing *Roberto Zucco*, a play about a man who
escaped both from high-security jails and from the
normal restrictions imposed by life in society. Although
Zucco is presented as a monster, he is also depicted as
compellingly attractive and very articulate when he
chooses – not unlike Brecht's Baal. His combination of
detachment and escapism, articulacy and self-denigration,
anguished isolation together with horror of society, all
this makes it tempting to see in him the spiritual self-
portrait of the author and a summation of his view of
himself vis-à-vis society.

Black Battles with Dogs

What is the value of a man's life? Is a European more
valuable than an African, or an engineer more useful than
a labourer? These are the questions at the centre of this
play. It starts with Alboury's simple statement: 'I have
come for the body.' The body he wants is that of a dead
worker, Alboury's brother or his friend, who has been
killed on the West African construction site where a road
bridge is being built, financed by European capital. Horn,
the site manager, tries to make a deal with him: he offers
him first whisky, then financial compensation; finally he
tries to put Alboury off with promises that the body will
be returned to his village the next morning. But Alboury
refuses to be put off and settles down to wait. In the
confrontation between Horn and Alboury, Koltès
presents the conflict of two opposing world views: Horn
is logical, managerial, sure of himself and of his ability to
get things done while Alboury is patient yet tenacious,
with an attitude towards the world that puts a value on
respect for the dead. For Horn a man is worth what he can

achieve when alive; for Alboury he takes his place in the natural cycle of the unborn, the living and the dead.

The second and third scenes of the play introduce the other two characters. In Scene 2 we meet Leonie, a young woman whom Horn has met on a recent trip to Paris and who has been persuaded to come out and visit him. She is suffering from a combination of travel sickness and culture shock and refuses to come out of the bungalow. But perhaps her main reason for shutting herself in is uncertainty about what is expected of her. In Scene 3 Cal appears. He is half Horn's age, a French engineer employed on the project. It slowly emerges that he is responsible for the death of the African worker and that he has dumped the body in a fit of panic.

The play's twenty short scenes are made up, almost exclusively, of encounters between just two out of these four characters, through which the playwright builds up a pattern of attraction and repulsion, desire and disgust, and reveals the ideological, political and economic foundations of the assumptions on which the characters base their behaviour. Koltès's use of extended monologue is strongly reminiscent of William Faulkner (a writer to whom Koltès acknowledged his debt), focusing on concrete, closely observed details, and employing a highly personal idiom. It is not remote from ordinary speech, yet posseses the complex, condensed quality of language in dreams, and lacks the realistic patina of banal, everyday talk.

The setting has a crucial role to play: the stage direction describes it as a construction site, somewhere in West Africa, surrounded by fences and observation towers, with housing for the site supervisors, clumps of bougainvillaea, a van pulled up under a tree and a half-finished bridge consisting of two concrete columns rising up from a sea of mud. The darkness, and the fact that the site is surrounded by armed guards, lends tension and suspense to a plot that has been set in motion by the death of one man and will end with the death of another. The violent atmosphere, the strained relationships between

Africans and Europeans, the fact that work on the project has come to a standstill and there are hints of financial corruption, all combine to undermine the value of such engineering projects funded by Western capital. The neo-colonialists are being engulfed by the former colony. Again, territory is a major issue.

Koltès claimed, however, that the play was not primarily about the effect of neo-colonialist economic policies on Black Africa, but rather about 'France and the Whites: something seen from a distance may become easier to decipher'.[7] By this he meant that the play focuses on the construction of European cultural identities. This can be seen in the conflict that pits Horn against Cal. Cal is an opportunist, a loner who cannot sustain relationships with others because he is emotionally immature. He accepts no moral claims and owes allegiance to nothing. His reason for taking work on Third World engineering projects is that they pay good money and enable him to parade his racial prejudices. He is coarse, self-pitying and fundamentally terrified of his own inadequacies. He is obsessed with status and with money and is driven by violent instincts that he cannot control.

Horn, on the other hand, is always self-controlled and reasonable: he knows what he is doing and why. He is completely loyal to the multi-national company that he works for, seing it almost as his family. He has a contempt for politics but is impressed by the way his company can function anywhere in the world, eluding the constraints of governments and their political or moral concerns. He is the perfect technician and organisation man, who makes it possible for such companies to function. He never questions the value of the engineering works that his company carries out in Third World countries, and a successfully completed bridge or a road gives him an almost sexual excitement, as he explains in Scene 10. In the contrast and conflict between these two characters,

[7] From Koltès's afterword, printed on the back cover of the Editions de Minuit publication of the play.

Koltès portrays mental attitudes that are characteristically Western (or white, or French). Although the African setting is significant, the same conflict could equally well be taking place in any 'underdeveloped' country.

The ideological foundation for Horn's behaviour emerges in his monologue at the end of Scene 4. In this, Horn describes his ideal solution to the problem of overpopulation, which is to construct an enormous city that would cover half of France, leaving the rest of the world free of human dwellings, so that its natural resources could be exploited for the benefit of all. His vision is at once grandiose and comic, revealing a very Western utopia, containing elements of generosity and egalitarianism, but fundamentally flawed, since it assumes that a Western (or, more specifically, French) model of civilisation is self-evidently the best for everyone, and since it depends for its realisation on a very high level of bureaucratic control.

This monologue follows another, by Alboury, in which he outlines a different concept altogether of how people may best live together in harmony. His vision is entirely based in the fraternal relationship he enjoyed with the dead man, and with the place that both occupied in their community. It also implies a metaphysical attitude, grounded in different principles: not so much organising and exploiting nature but more responding to it, attentive to the interrelationship of humans, their communities and the environment that sustains them. Above all, Alboury's monologue reveals an awareness of the fragility of any state of harmony that human beings may achieve, whereas Horn is quite unconscious of the deep irony in his laying down the law about an ideal society when he cannot even manage to keep the peace in this small encampment.

In French the euphemism often used to describe projects such as the one on which Horn and Cal are engaged is 'la co-opération'. Horn believes that their relationship with the African country is, effectively, a cooperative one; Cal, much more cynical, is clear that he is simply there to display his technological superiority and take what he can. In reality, as the play gradually reveals, both are in contradiction with the situation in which they are placed. Far from being in a position of strength or superiority both are in fact impotent. Horn is impotent to meet the simple demand of Alboury and this impotence is matched at the sexual level by his failure to prevent Leonie from drifting away from him and becoming fascinated by Alboury. Cal, despite an apparent display of strength in killing the worker, is terrified of the consequences of his action. He has spent the evening dragging the body from one hiding place to another, finally dumping it in the cesspit. He is powerless to prevent the inevitable outcome, when he pays the price with his own death.

The other two characters, Leonie and Alboury, are both more enigmatic. In Alboury's case this is not only because of his different world-view but also a consequence of his use of the white man's language. The French in which he expresses himself is correct but basic: it is the second language imposed by the neo-colonial relationship. Horn and Cal make use of language at a sophisticated level, to justify themselves, to explain, to deceive, to bargain, to manoeuvre. Alboury's words are different: they carry concrete, unequivocal meanings, without hidden implications. He has come for the body; if he doesn't get it, he will retaliate. This is his consistent position throughout the play. Leonie is very different, though sharing something with Alboury. She is a 'poor white', flown out from France at Horn's expense and for his entertainment. She has not been prepared for what she finds: everything in the African setting is strange to her. However, as an Alsacienne, she has also learned to communicate in a second language (German) and her solution to Alboury speaking Woloff is to speak German with him. Koltès expressed their relationship by saying:

Leonie sees in the black a way of bearing her condemnation ... She sees the blacks as people who carry their condemnation on their faces ... That of the blacks seems enviable to her, she would like to change places, her burden seems heavier and, especially, more idiotic.[8]

When Leonie, in Scene 12, scarifies her cheeks, she is partly expressing the feelings of worthlessness imposed upon her by the men, but also a desire for escape into a different condition. The 'condemnation' Koltès refers to includes both the racist attitudes expressed towards Alboury and the sexist attitudes from which Leonie suffers.

Ultimately, the strength and originality of Koltès's work lies in its manipulation of language. It would be wrong to take any of the characters in this play too literally, as if they were accurate depictions of real people one might meet on a West African building site. Koltès's whole approach to theatre, at once very formal, very violent and very down-to-earth, has a lot in common with that of Jean Genet. Genet frequently insisted that the theatre cannot deal with the problems of real life, just as Koltès considered it to be 'the opposite of life' (see p. xv). Like Genet before him, Koltès uses the freedom that this view of theatre implies in order to develop a meditation on subjectivity and point of view. The audience is constantly being made to see how one point of view conditions another and how the construction of subjectivity is a constant struggle.

In *Black Battles with Dogs*, Koltès shows us, not black and white images of the real world, but the sombre, shaded phantoms that we try to externalise and impose on others but which, ultimately, are bound to return to haunt, and possibly to destroy us. The battle takes place, in the last analysis, at the imaginary or ideological level. Linked to this concern with the imagination and construction of identity, is the playwright's comment that the right question to ask of a play is not *why* the characters do what they do, or say what they say, but *how*.

People too often tend, when you tell them a story, to ask

[8] *Alternatives Théâtrales*, op. cit., p. 18.

the question 'why?' whereas I think the only question worth asking is 'how?'[9]

Taking his cue from this attitude, Chéreau quoted Brecht's preface to *In the Jungle of Cities* for the programme of *Dans la solitude des champs de coton*:

Don't worry your heads about the motives for the fight, concentrate on the stakes. Judge impartially the technique of the contenders and keep your eyes fixed on the finish.[10]

The vocabulary used here (stakes, fight, contenders, etc.) recurs frequently in Koltès's own statements about his plays. The technique of the contenders is as much verbal as physical, and as they fight to the finish, they reveal to us how our ideas are constructed through the many-layered texture of the linguistic and imaginary reality we inhabit.

Return to the Desert

In this play, Koltès returned to the main theme of much of his early work: the family – its inbred conflict and its links with property, inheritance, ownership. In earlier works such as *L'Héritage* or *Sallinger*, Koltès had used the family as the basic social unit within which both agreement and dissent, belonging and rejection could be expressed. In ways that recall both Faulkner and Salinger, Koltès presents individuals who may feel alienated within the family structure, but who return to it as the only environment in which they can discover self-definition. *L'Héritage* owed a particular debt to Faulkner's *As I Lay Dying* and the characteristic Faulknerian probing of the ties that bind yet frustrate the members of a family is again evident in *Return to the Desert*. An additional Faulknerian characteristic is the way in which

[9] 'Un Hangar à l'ouest', op. cit., p. 115.

[10] *Brecht Collected Plays: One*, Methuen, 1994, p. 118.

the family relationships mirror the racial tensions in society outside and beyond the intimate family space.

The play opens on a pitched battle between Mathilde and her brother Adrien. It is November 1960; Mathilde is fifty-two, Adrien fifty. They are the last survivors of a bourgeois family which had made a fortune from the expansion of the Lorraine steel industry in the early years of the century, but can now do nothing to delay its decline, lacking the energy or imagination needed to diversify into other kinds of manufacturing. Because she never behaved like a proper bourgeoise in her youth, Mathilde has been victimised by her brother and his friends: after the Liberation of France in 1945, she was accused of sleeping with the Germans and paraded through Metz with her hair shaved off. She fled to Algeria to build a new life, where she brought up her two children, Fatima and Edouard. Now she is once again fleeing from hostilities (in Algeria) and returns to confront Adrien in the family home.

The saga of a family dynasty is not new, but the linking of a provincial industrial family to the Algerian war has considerable originality. For while the Second World War and German occupation of France have provided material for hundreds of plays and films, very few dramatists have dealt with the equally disturbing material of the Algerian war. And yet this conflict, which lasted from 1954 until 1962, cost over 100,000 dead or wounded, and affected the lives of everyone living in France or in the French North African colonies.

Koltès never wrote 'issue' plays in the straightforward sense. His method of handling social and political concerns was always oblique. Just as he insisted that *Black Battles with Dogs* was not a play about neo-colonialism, so *Return* is not directly about the Algerian war. Rather, it deals with attitudes and social realities which both explain and are explained by the conflict in Algeria. It concerns itself with the mentalities current in the early 1960s in a provincial town such as Metz, and the action of the play develops a rich interweaving of the characters' dreams and aspirations, their behaviour in the private spaces of the home, and their actions in the society outside. In fact a principal theme of the play is how the French managed to deny the reality of the war going on in Algeria. Implied within this is the question of ownership – not only of colonial territories, but of France, of national heritage, of the right to space, both physical and ideological.

The linguistic texture of the play has a condensed, calculated quality, designed to ensure that even the most banal exchanges between the characters bring into play a whole range of cultural and ideological values. Because the social background of the characters is more carefully established than in *Black Battles with Dogs*, their speeches are closer to realistic, everyday dialogue than those of the earlier play. Nevertheless, they retain a strong imprint of their author's original approach to dramatic dialogue, including virtuoso passages of monologue, and many places where what is being voiced in the play is clearly their thoughts, anxieties or nightmares, rather than anything they would readily say to one another in ordinary, everyday speech. Moreover, there are passages of the play that remind us of the fundamental opposition to real life in Koltès's theatre referred to above (p. xv), such as Scene 17, in which Edouard 'takes off'.

The action of the play covers a period of roughly nine months, during which Adrien and Mathilde squabble over everything as they did when they were children. But now their fighting has a life-and-death seriousness: through her daughter, Mathilde makes contact again with her dead childhood friend Marie, and becomes convinced that she was murdered by Adrien. Mathilde wreaks vengeance on Adrien's friends (who now make up the ruling class in Metz) for their share in her humiliation in 1945. Her daughter, Fatima, becomes pregnant in similar circumstances to those of her mother, and gives birth to half-caste twins. Finally both sister and brother realise that they have no future in Metz and they leave together for a life of retirement wandering around the spa towns of the world, forever in exile.

The dialogue, although less declamatory than that of *Black Battles with Dogs*, still manages to combine the tone of both private and public discourse. This can be seen in the opening scene, where Mathilde and Adrien confront one another for the first time in fifteen years. Their argument has resonances of all the childhood squabbles which neither has forgotten, while also confronting adult matters such as property and inheritance. In addition, the formal tone and the length of their speeches gives to their exchange the quality of something belonging to myth or ritual, and this is further strengthened by the elements of Arabic culture introduced by Koltès. The play opens with a sequence in Arabic, its sections are named after the divisions of the Muslim day, and one of its central characters (Fatima) is half Arabic. In this way, the North African world is constantly present as a defining framework, ignored by most of the characters, but no less present for that.

Relationships between the French and the Arab community in Metz are dealt with explicitly in the scenes involving affairs outside the limits of the house. These are where Koltès makes most use of humour, with two distinct aspects of the plot, which come together in the end. The first concerns Edouard's desperate attempts to find the red-light district of the town. It turns out to be in the Arab quarter and Aziz, the Arab servant, agrees somewhat unwillingly to take him there. Meanwhile, the audience has seen Adrien and his cronies scheming to plant a bomb in the very café in the Arab quarter to which Aziz is taking Mathieu and Edouard. The scenes in which the scheme is hatched (Scenes 9 and 16) are broadly farcical, and strongly reminiscent of similar scenes in the adventures of the cartoon hero Tintin. Patrice Chéreau claimed that Koltès was a life-long admirer of *Tintin*:

> *Le Retour au désert* was a play that was deliberately funny, and *Roberto Zucco* is also a very funny play. Bernard Koltès wanted people to laugh, at a profound level. He adored [...] *Tintin* by Hergé. He had a

profound admiration for the dramaturgical skill of *Tintin*, and used to say that, as scenarios, the *Tintin* stories were masterpieces, all of them. In *Le Retour au désert*, there are four speeches borrowed directly from Hergé. And there are also speeches like that in *Roberto Zucco*.[11]

Setting out to write a play with a lighter, more humorous touch, he seems to have taken inspiration from *Tintin*, and one can easily imagine Borny, Sablon the Préfet, and Plantières the Police Chief drawn by the Belgian cartoonist Hergé, exuding self-satisfaction, cowardice and racism in equal measures. Even the appearance (in Scene 11) of the mysterious 'Great Black Parachutist' has a comic side to it: that he should be black underlines the puzzlement of Adrien and the threat that he feels, as a propertied bourgeois, from the army that is supposed to defend his values. The Great Black Parachutist represents everything that Adrien depends on, and yet, at the same time, everything that he fears. Into the monologue by the Parachutist, which concludes this scene, Koltès deliberately infiltrates some phrases from a speech by de Gaulle about the impossible nostalgia felt by the French for their former colonial role; spoken by a soldier who originates from the colonies, this has an extra ironic resonance.

The structure of *Return to the Desert* has an open, almost epic quality. The three plays Koltès wrote before it – *Black Battles with Dogs, Western Dock, In the Solitude of the Cotton Fields* – all take place in the course of one or two nights; *Return to the Desert* covers more than nine months. The reason for the difference seems to lie in his encounter with Shakespeare: his translation of *A Winter's Tale*, completed just before he wrote *Return to the Desert*, had, by his own admission, opened his eyes to a new kind of structural liberty available to the playwright. In his earlier plays he had adopted the neo-classical conventions

[11] Public interview at the Edinburgh Festival, August 1995, published in *Theatre Forum*, 9, Summer/Fall 1996, pp. 12–18.

of the French dramatic tradition, with its respect for the three unities (of time, place and action). He had shown that he could structure an intense, tightly knotted situation. For his last two plays, he decided to experiment with a much freer, more episodic structure. *Return to the Desert* reads like a transitional play: it has passages of violent intensity where monologues are thrown backwards and forwards between the characters as if they were bombs about to explode. But there are also sections of the play in which the action shifts rapidly from one place to another, with the broader sweep of epic theatre; when he came to write his last play, *Roberto Zucco*, Koltès was to make even more thorough use of the epic structure.

Roberto Zucco

Koltès's anti-hero Roberto Zucco is a character whose mythical dimensions are more outsize than any of his previous dramatic characters. He walks free over the roof of the high-security prison in which he had been held; he quotes passages of Victor Hugo; his death at the end of the play is heralded by a hurricane and an explosion in the heavens 'as blinding as an atomic bomb'. He was described by the author as 'a mythical character, a hero like Samson or Goliath, monsters of strength, finally struck down by a stone or a woman'.[12] And yet, paradoxically, this is also the most realistic of Koltès's plays, in which the dialogue is closest to everyday speech (while nevertheless retaining a certain poetic density that recalls Brecht's *Baal*).

Koltès first became interested in the case of Roberto Succo in 1988, when he saw a 'wanted' poster on the metro carrying photographs of him. Succo had murdered both parents and had been given a life sentence in Italy in 1981. After five years he had been given parole, had

[12] Afterword printed on the back cover of the Editions de Minuit publication.

broken it and had been at liberty for nearly two years, committing in that time a string of other offences, including the murder of a police inspector, before being recaptured (as a result of a tip-off from a girl). Back in prison, in Treviso, he gave his guards the slip just long enough to climb onto the prison roof, where he remained for some time, throwing tiles and shouting to the assembled journalists, before being recaptured. Shortly afterwards he committed suicide. Koltès saw the pictures of Succo's final defiant hours on the roof of the prison when they were broadcast on the television news, and was fascinated by the way the media portrayed him. The first thing that had struck him about the 'wanted' poster was that it included four different portraits of Succo: 'each one showed a face that was so different from the others that you had to look several times before you could be sure it was the same person.'[13]

In creating his dramatic character Zucco, Koltès altered significant details in the life of Succo: for example, Succo killed both his mother and his father before his first term in prison, whereas Koltès's Zucco has already killed his father before the play starts, and it is only in the second scene, after his escape from prison, that he murders his mother. Koltès depicts Zucco's life as taking place in a kind of labyrinth, where nothing is quite what it seems. Above all, he offers us a Zucco who never appears quite the same from one scene to the next. Like the photos on the 'wanted' poster, like the images of the real Succo broadcast by the media, each depiction of Zucco is different, depending on the perspective from which he is seen, and the person who is doing the looking. Koltès has used a method of free association in constructing the play. Certain details are inspired by things said by the real Succo – the bird imagery in the play, for example, would seem to derive from a tape of Succo's voice in which he said: 'Sooner or later we all have to die. All. And that's what makes the birds sing, the birds, that makes the bees

---

[13] *Alternatives Théâtrales*, op. cit., p. 41.

sing, that makes the birds laugh.'[14] Other details come from Koltès's own experience, such as the metro, with the poster, which is the setting for Scene 6.

The play is prefaced by an extract from an ancient ritual of the cult of Mithras, quoted by Jung in the last interview he gave to the BBC, and it manages to combine throughout the action resonances of a mythical and psychoanalytical kind, as well as the brutal realities of the Succo murders. The crimes committed by the central character do not become the subject of an 'investigation' (as in a detective thriller) nor of an explanation (as in a psychological thriller). In common with some English playwrights, such as Edward Bond, Koltès clearly felt that violence was one of the defining features of our society: one that we try not to see and that should not be explained away. The play concerns itself as much with the attitudes towards violence in society as with the monstrous nature of Zucco's actions. Koltès goes to some pains to avoid judging Zucco's behaviour.

Zucco himself seems unsure of his own identity: he is unwilling to reveal his name to the girl in Scene 3, he longs for reincarnation as a dog in Scene 8, and it is not until the police officers have him cornered in Scene 14 that he is able to identify himself: 'I'm the murderer of my father, my mother, a police sergeant, and a child. I'm a killer.' Koltès clearly believed that any one of us is capable of becoming a killer:

There are times when I, too, almost feel like killing. [...] All it needs is a slight trigger movement, something like an epileptic fit in Dostoevsky [...] When I am told that I have sung the praises of a murderer, or something like that, because that's what will be said, I shall say that he is an exemplary killer, in the sense that

<hr />

[14] Ibid.

I think he is like everyone, in so far as it's only a matter of a small release.[15]

This belief does not, however, lead him to present his subject in the light of a psychoanalytic 'case study'. In the opening dialogue of the play, the parodic discussion between the first and second prison officers makes it clear that we should not expect explanations of either a Freudian kind (the second officer is convinced it's all to do with sex) nor of a conventional moral kind (the first officer says: 'it's sheer evil' – in French: '*pure vice*'). The play rejects entirely the traditional dualism between conscious and sub-conscious in favour of a concept of transparency. Zucco himself speaks of being transparent in Scene 6, and his whole strategy is to avoid being identified. From Scene 8 until the end of the play, he reluctantly acquires an identity, but it is as a figment of other people's imaginations.

This appears most clearly in Scene 10, the longest of the play, which takes place in a public park. Here Zucco takes two hostages, a woman and her young son. The dramatisation of the episode lays emphasis on the role of the bystanders, their voyeuristic fascination with the events enacted before their eyes, their desire for a juicy crime, and their need to demonise Zucco as the young hooligan. For Peter Stein, the play's first director, this scene shows how, in the television age,

the public needs to 'have an experience'. The poor criminals end up in the role of victims: they become the actors performing, doing a job of work required by everyone else.[16]

Each bystander has a different explanation of what is going on, but far from explaining the dilemma of the woman, the child, or Zucco, they simply tell us about

[15] Quoted by Jean-Marc Lantéri in 'Le Cran d'arrêt Koltésien', *Séquence* 2, Théâtre National de Strasbourg, 1995, pp. 32–3.

[16] *Alternatives Théâtrales*, op. cit., p. 53.

their own mentalities. Their superficial explanations of criminal conduct remind the audience of the 'rationalisations' for Zucco's behaviour offered by the comic duo who appeared in the first scene as prison warders, and who return in Scene 14 as policemen. Their bumbling discussions recall the two identical detectives Dupont and Dupond in the *Tintin* stories, who always get the wrong end of the stick.

The thirst for violence in contemporary society is further demonstrated in the family relationships the play depicts. The family introduced in Scene 3 is one in which every relationship is based on brutality: husband to wife, parent to child, brother to sister. The brother's attitude towards his sister is especially instrumental. For him, there are only two options: either he protects her virginity or (once she has lost it) he sells her to a pimp. Her relationship with Zucco, by contrast, has a different quality: they meet as equals, each putting themselves in the hands of the other. She gives herself to him, but he also places himself at her mercy, and it is in fact she who, later on, betrays him to the police.

The play relies more on dialogue and less on monologue than his earlier work, and it moves freely from one location to another. It is set in an unnamed French town, which recalls the urban jungle of Brecht's early plays, especially since the red-light district, in which many of the scenes take place, is known as 'Little Chicago'. The titles Koltès gave to the scenes suggest what happens in them rather than their location. For example, the scene in which the girl betrays Zucco is headed 'Delilah' and the one in which her brother sells her to the pimp is headed 'The Deal'. The play's time-scale is vague: it covers the period between Zucco's first escape from prison and his final, fatal fall from the prison roof, but the number of days involved is unclear: it could be as little as two or three, or it could be a matter of weeks.

If *Roberto Zucco* seems quite different from most of Koltès's earlier plays, it is also because of a new note of intimacy in the interpersonal relationships it depicts. Without sacrificing his emphasis on *the deal* and on the commercial trade-offs that dominate so much of our lives, the author seems to have overcome some of the distaste he had previously felt for the depiction of a relationship of love or affection. This is particularly clear in the monologue of the sister, Scene 13, entitled 'Ophelia'. The language has not lost its condensed, poetic quality, so that the listener is conscious that it says things, not only about the particular relationship involved, but also about all sexual relationships. But where, in the earlier plays, these additional resonances carried echoes of ideological concerns, in *Roberto Zucco* they relate mainly to the war of the sexes and to the gamut of emotions that ranges from desire to disgust.

The quotation from Jung indicates Koltès's growing interest in placing these themes within a universal mythical context. The mythic quality of Zucco's actions is partly a function of their very excess. At the opening of the play, Zucco has already killed his father; in the second scene he strangles his mother. In the most graphic way possible, he has thus destroyed his own origins. His three further crimes are rape (destruction of innocence), murder of a policeman (destruction of the law) and, finally, the murder of a child (destruction of the future). Zucco is beyond the understanding of an audience: he incarnates the cosmic cruelty that has a quality of indifference to it, central to the Artaudian concept of cruelty. He never succeeds in establishing contact with another character in the play (with the possible exception of the girl): his desperate monologue on the telephone in Scene 8, with no one at the other end, is an emblem of his situation. The text encourages us to think of him in a mythical light, with constant references to the labyrinth and to the myths of Theseus and of Icarus. His wanderings around the city suggest the search for a way out of the labyrinth; his encounters with the bruiser suggest the combat with the Minotaur; and his final appearance on the roof and fall from sight in a blinding light suggest the escape and death of Icarus, from flying too close to the sun.

Jean-Marc Lantéri, one of the few critics to have made a detailed study of Koltès's work, concludes that this play presents a kind of oscillation between Eastern and Western values. He points out that Koltès's mature plays almost all contain passages of text drawn from non-Western cultural sources (Woloff in *Black Battles with Dogs*; Quechua in *Western Dock*; Islamic in *Return to the Desert*; the Mithras Liturgy in *Roberto Zucco*). He suggests that Koltès was, in the words of his German translator Simon Werle, 'not entirely inserted in Western culture'.[17] Undoubtedly Koltès never felt at ease with his own background and spent a great deal of his energies in searching for ways of escape. He was a spiritual nomad, incapable of settling in any one ideology. From this he derived the detachment necessary to criticise the stresses and strains of late twentieth-century Western society. But it also prevented him from constructing any coherent alternative. The final, haunting image we are left with from his last play is that of a man with a death-wish, destroyed by something within him which he never completely understands. This is drama pushed to the amoral limits of Quentin Tarantino's screenplays.

Production history

During his lifetime Koltès was disappointed that his plays were so seldom revived in France after their first production by Patrice Chéreau (see Chronology). He also expressed regret that his plays were not performed

---

[17] Jean-Marc Lantéri has made a psychoanalytic study of Koltès's work (presented as a doctoral thesis to the University of Lille, 1995); he has also published two articles on *Roberto Zucco*: 'L'Oiseau et le labyrinthe' in *Alternatives Théâtrales*, pp. 42–6, and 'Le Cran d'arrêt Koltésien' in *Séquence 2*, Théâtre National de Strasbourg, 1995, pp. 29–33. The quotation by Simon Werle (who has translated most of Koltès's plays into German) is from an interview in *Alternatives Théâtrales*, pp. 99–100.

more frequently in Britain. Yet the production history of *Black Battles with Dogs* shows how, in the early 1980s, he suddenly acquired a reputation, in both Paris and New York, as the most promising new French playwright. The play's world première, at the La Mama Theatre of New York, was produced by Françoise Kourilsky. Shortly before this, Kourilsky had set up the Ubu Repertory Theatre in New York, funded by French government subsidy, with the purpose of providing a shop window in America for new French playwrights. Koltès's fascination with New York made it inevitable that he would meet Kourilsky, and she was keen to make his work known in the USA. The translator, Matthew Ward, succeeded in capturing some of the quality of Koltès's original style, and his use of American English was peculiarly appropriate to the international world inhabited by Horn and Cal in this play. The first production was a relatively small-scale affair, and there is no record of what Koltès felt about it.

The first production in France, however, was a different matter. For the opening production of his new directorship at the Théâtre des Amandiers in 1983, Chéreau wanted to make a splash, and he succeeded. He brought with him to Nanterre the Italian designer Richard Peduzzi, with whom he had already worked for more than a decade, both in Lyons at the Théâtre National Populaire, and at the Bayreuth Theatre for his celebrated staging of Wagner's *Ring* cycle in the late 1970s, conducted by Pierre Boulez. His design for *Black Battles with Dogs* followed the stage directions closely, with two unfinished concrete bridge supports rising out of sight and clumps of bushes planted in the heaps of sand and rubble strewn across the stage. But instead of the bungalow, there was a caravan, towed on and off stage by a car, at various stages of the action. The parts of Horn and Cal were taken by Michel Piccoli and Philippe Léotard, two actors well known to French audiences, especially from their work for the cinema. Leonie was performed by Myriam Boyer and Alboury by Sidiki Bakaba. The play was favourably

received by the critics, who were unanimous in their praise
for all aspects of the production – acting, design and
direction – as well as for the text.

The play was quickly taken up by theatres in Germany,
with four productions (at Frankfurt, Tübingen, Wup-
pertal and Munich) before the end of 1984 and a further
eighteen in the ensuing ten years. The first production in
England was by Michael Batz at the Gate Theatre,
Notting Hill, in 1988. The Scottish première was at the
Traverse Theatre, Edinburgh, for the Edinburgh
International Festival in 1991, directed by Andrew
Farrell. Both productions used the translation by
Matthew Ward, published by Methuen in *New French
Plays*, 1989. The author himself always expressed
dissatisfaction with this translation and so, for this
collection, a new translation has been made by David
Bradby and Maria M. Delgado.

For *Return to the Desert*, Koltès wanted the première to
be in central Paris rather than at Nanterre. Much as he
admired Chéreau, he felt that his association with him
was leading him to be seen as a playwright whose work
was 'difficult' and strictly for the rather self-consciously
cultivated audience that attended avant-garde theatre. He
was keen for his work to appeal to a broader public, and
had written the main role of Mathilde especially for
Jacqueline Maillan, a popular performer with her own
following, who specialised in boulevard comedy and
seldom appeared in a 'serious' play. Accordingly, the
production, directed by Chéreau, and sponsored by the
Théâtre des Amandiers, took place at the Théâtre du
Rond-Point, in the centre of Paris in 1988. However, the
production was not greeted with the same acclaim as
Black Battles with Dogs. The comedy in the text was not
successfully realised, and the audience appears to have
found the production puzzling. According to Chéreau,
this was because Jacqueline Maillan's audience expected a
traditional boulevard comedy and were perplexed by the
play, whereas those Nanterre habitués who attended felt

that Koltès and Chéreau were selling out. Koltès himself helped to muddy the waters by complaining about the world première of the play in Hamburg, directed by Alexander Lang, accusing it of being *too* lightweight. It was not until Jacques Nichet's revival in 1995 that the play received the comic performance it deserves and the critics agreed on the merits of the play. The role of Mathilde in this production was taken by Myriam Boyer, who had played Leonie in the 1983 production of *Black Battles with Dogs*.

My translation, published in this volume, was commissioned by Midnight Theatre Company and made possible by an Arts Council award. Its director, Derek Wax, produced a staged reading at the Traverse Theatre, Edinburgh, in 1993, with Sîan Phillips as Mathilde, and Patrick Godfrey as Adrien.

Roberto Zucco received its world première in German at the Berlin Schaubühne, directed by Peter Stein in April 1990, a year after the author's death. Koltès had specifically asked Stein to produce the play, having seen and admired his production of Chekhov's *Three Sisters*. Stein said that he had fallen in love with the play, despite not being attracted to Koltès's earlier work. He felt that in *Roberto Zucco*, for the first time, Koltès had overcome his tendency to write in an excessively literary style, and had created a genuinely dramatic structure. In the four years following Stein's première, there were another sixteen new productions of the play in theatres throughout Germany. The French première was directed by Bruno Boeglin at the Théâtre National Populaire, Villeurbanne, on 7 November 1991, and has been followed by several further productions, including one at the Théâtre National de Strasbourg, directed by Jean-Louis Martinelli, in March 1995. In addition to this, the play has been performed in Austria, Canada, Colombia, Denmark, Spain, Finland, Hungary, Italy, Norway, Holland, Poland, Romania, Russia, Switzerland, the Czech Republic and Venezuela.

The translation by Martin Crimp published in this volume was commissioned by the Royal Court Theatre for a production planned for 1997 directed by James Macdonald. The play was also broadcast on BBC Radio 3 in June 1996 in a translation by David Zane Mairowitz.

David Bradby
Royal Holloway
University of London, 1996

Black Battles
with Dogs

Combat de nègre
et de chiens

translated by DAVID BRADBY *and*
MARIA M. DELGADO

The first production of *Black Battles with Dogs* (then entitled *Come Dog, Come Night*) was given in Matthew Ward's American translation by Ubu Repertory Theatre at La Mama in New York on 9 December 1982 with the following cast:

Horn	Louis Zorich
Alboury	Afemo
Leonie	Barbara eda-Young
Cal	Ron Frazier

Directed by Françoise Kourilsky
Designed by Roberto Moscoso
Lighting by Beverly Emmons
Music by Aiyb Dieng and Teko Manong

The British première (entitled *Struggle of the Black Man and the Dogs*) was directed by Michael Batz at the Gate Theatre, London, on 6 June 1988, with the following cast:

Horn	Keith Hazemore
Alboury	Roy Lee
Leonie	Josephine Welcome
Cal	Jonathan Oliver

Designed by Cathy Ryan

In a West African country, anywhere from Senegal to Nigeria, a construction site for a public works project of a foreign company.

Characters

Horn, *sixty years old, site foreman*
Alboury, *a black man who has mysteriously gained entry to the camp*
Leonie, *a woman brought by Horn*
Cal, *an engineer in his thirties*

Setting

The camp where the managers live and materials are stored, surrounded by fences and surveillance towers:
  – a clump of bougainvillaea; a van parked under a tree;
  – a veranda, table and rocking-chair, whisky;
  – a door of one of the bungalows half open.

The construction site: a river runs through it; an uncompleted bridge; in the distance, a lake.

The calls of the guards: sounds of tongues and throats, of iron striking iron, iron striking wood, faint cries, gasps, whistling, brief chants which stream over the barbed wire like laughter or coded messages, blocking out the sounds of the bush surrounding the camp.

The bridge: two symmetrical constructions, white and gigantic, of concrete and cables, which rise up out of the red sand, but do not meet, in a huge empty sky above a river of mud.

'He called the child born to him in exile *Nouofia*, which means "conceived in the desert".'
Alboury: king of the Duiloff (Woloff) in the nineteenth century who opposed white incursion.
Toubab: common name for whites in certain regions of Africa.

'The jackal pounces on an abandoned carcass, greedily tears off a few mouthfuls, eats on the run, untrappable and unrepentant scavenger, sometime killer.'

'Along both coasts of the Cape, it was certain death, and in the middle, a mountain of ice, to which the blind who ran into it would be condemned.'

'Throughout the long suffocation of her victim, in a meditative and ritual ecstasy, obscurely, the lioness remembers the possessions of love.'

Scene 1

Behind the bougainvillaea, at twilight.

Horn I thought I saw someone, from over there, behind the tree.

Alboury I am Alboury, sir; I have come for the body; his mother came to the site to lay branches on the body, sir, but she found nothing; and if the body is not given to her, his mother will wander through the village, wailing, all night long. A terrible night, sir, nobody will be able to sleep because of the old woman's cries: that is why I am here.

Horn Was it the police or the village that sent you?

Alboury I am Alboury; I have come for my brother's body, sir.

Horn It's a terrible affair; a bad fall; unfortunately a truck came speeding through; the driver will be punished. The workers are careless, despite the strict instructions they're given. You'll have the body tomorrow; it must have been taken to the infirmary to be tidied up before being properly presented to the family. Please give them my condolences. My condolences to you too. What a sad business.

Alboury It is both sad and not sad. If he had not been a worker, sir, the family would have buried the gourd in the ground and said: one less mouth to feed. It's still one less mouth to feed, the site will soon close, and he would then no longer be a worker, sir. Then it would have been another mouth to feed. So it's only sad for a little while, sir.

Horn I've not seen you round here before. Have a whisky, come out from behind the tree, I can hardly see you. Come and sit down at the table, Alboury. Here, on the site, we have a good relationship with the police and the local authorities; I'm proud of that.

Alboury Since the site was opened, the village has been talking about you. So I said: here is my chance to see the white man up close. I still have much to learn, sir, and I said to my soul: run to my ears and listen, run up to my eyes and do not forget anything you see.

Horn Well, your command of French is to be admired; and no doubt you're equally at ease in English and in other languages too; you have a real talent for languages. Are you a civil servant? You have something of that air. And you know more than you let on. Well now, that's turned into quite a string of compliments.

Alboury It is a useful way to start.

Horn It's strange. Usually the village sends out a delegation and things are settled quite quickly. It's normally fast and formal: eight or ten people, eight or ten brothers of the dead man; I'm used to quick settlements. Sad about your brother: you call everybody 'brother' here. The family will want compensation; we'll give it to them, of course, give it to the rightful party, as long as they don't get carried away. But you, I'm sure I've never seen you before.

Alboury I have only come to collect the body, sir, and I will leave as soon as I have it.

Horn Yes, yes yes, the body! You'll get it tomorrow. Forgive my anxiety, I've a lot on my mind. My wife's just arrived; she's been unpacking her things for hours, I don't even know what she thinks of the place. It's a big change having a woman here; I'm not used to it.

Alboury It is very good to have a woman here.

Horn I'm only recently married; very very recently; in fact, I can tell you that it hasn't even been finalised yet, I mean all the formalities. But marriage is still a big change. I'm not used to this sort of thing; it stresses me, and the

fact that she's still in her room is making me nervous;
she's still in there, she's still in there, she's been arranging
her things for hours. Let's have a whisky while we're
waiting, I'll introduce you to her; we'll have a little party
and then you can stay. Come over to the table; there's not
much light here. You know, my eyes aren't what they
used to be. Come here where I can have a look at you.

Alboury   Impossible, sir. Look at the guards, look at
them, up there. They are watching the camp inside and
out, they are watching me, sir. If they see me sit down
with you, they will be suspicious; they will say never trust
a live goat in the lion's den. Do not be offended by what
they say. It is more honourable to be a lion than a goat.

Horn   But they let you in. Normally unless you're some
official representative, you need a pass. They know that.

Alboury   They know that the old woman cannot be left
to cry all night and tomorrow; she must be calmed; the
village cannot be kept awake, the body must be given to
the mother. They know very well why I am here.

Horn   We will have it brought to you tomorrow. In the
meantime, my head's killing me, I need a whisky.
Alboury, don't you think it's silly for an old man like me
to have taken a wife?

Alboury   Women are not silly. They do say that the
best soup comes from old pots. Do not be offended by
what they say. They have their own way of doing things,
but it is a great honour for you.

Horn   Even getting married?

Alboury   Above all getting married. First you pay the
price, and then you don't let go.

Horn   You're a wise man! I think she's coming. Come
here, come on, talk to me. Here are the glasses. You can't
stay behind that tree, in the dark. Come and join me.

Alboury   I cannot sir. My eyes cannot take the glare;

they blink and burn; they are not used to the strong lights you have at night.

Horn   Come over, come over, then you'll be able to see her.

Alboury   I will see her from a distance.

Horn   My head's killing me, Alboury. What can she have been doing for this long? I want to know what she thinks. Do you know what the surprise is? All these problems! I'm putting on a fireworks display later this evening; stay; it's an indulgence which cost me a fortune. Then we'll talk about this other business. Yes, there's always been a very good understanding; I've got the authorities in my pocket. When I think that she's behind that door, there, and I don't even know what she's thinking. If you're from the police, all the better. I'm always glad to work with them. Africa must be quite a shock for a woman who's never left Paris. The fireworks will be quite something. And I'll go and see what's happened to that damned corpse. (*He goes out.*)

Scene 2

Horn (*in front of the half-open door*)   Leonie, are you ready?

Leonie   I'm tidying up. (**Horn** *approaches.*) No, I'm not tidying up. (**Horn** *stops.*) I'm waiting till it stops moving.

Horn   What?

Leonie   Till it stops moving. It'll be better when it's dark; it's the same at night in Paris: I always feel sad for about an hour, at the time when day passes into night. Besides, even babies cry when the sun goes down. I mustn't forget to take my pills; it's important. (*She sticks her head half-way out of the door and points to the bougainvillaea.*) What are these flowers called?

Horn   I don't know. (*She disappears again.*) Come and
have a whisky.

Leonie   A whisky? Oh dear, no; that's taboo. That's all I
need, you'd really see something then. No, strictly taboo.

Horn   Come out anyway.

Leonie   I'm making a list of what's missing; I'm missing
a lot of things and I've a lot of other things I don't need.
Everybody told me to bring a jumper, Africa's cold at
night; cold, oh, the swines. So now I've got three jumpers
on my hands. I'm not very well. I'm scared, Cookie, really
scared. What are the other men like? People don't usually
like me very much at first.

Horn   There's only one other man here, I've already
told you that.

Leonie   Flying, now there's something I don't like.
Really, I prefer the phone; one can always hang up. But I
prepared myself, prepared like crazy; I listened to reggae
all bloody day, the other people in the house were going
bonkers. Do you know what I discovered when I opened
my suitcase? Parisians really smell; I knew it; this stench,
I've smelt it in the metro, on the streets, on people you
brush against, I've smelt it hanging and rotting in
corners. And I can still smell it, there, in my suitcase; I
can't stand it any longer. When a jumper, a blouse, any
little piece of cloth gets the stench of fish and chips or the
odour of a hospital, you try and get it out; well this smell's
even worse. It'll take ages to air all my clothes. Oh, I'm so
glad to be here. Africa, at last!

Horn   But you haven't seen anything yet, and you won't
even come out of your room.

Leonie   Oh, I've seen enough and I can see enough from
here to love it. I'm not just a tourist. I'm ready now; as
soon as I finish my list of what's missing and what I have
too much of, and when I've aired these clothes, I'll come
right out, I promise.

Horn   I'll wait for you, Leonie.

Leonie   No, don't wait for me, don't wait. (*The calls of the guards;* **Leonie** *partially appears.*) What was that?

Horn   It's the guards. From time to time, they call out to each other at night, it helps them to keep awake.

Leonie   It's terrible. (*She listens.*) Don't wait for me. (*She goes back inside.*) Oh Cookie, I have a confession to make.

Horn   What?

Leonie (*softly*)   Just before leaving last night, I took a walk along the Pont Neuf. And do you know what? I suddenly felt happy, so happy like never before, for no reason. When anything like that happens, well, I know something bad's coming. I don't like dreaming about happy things or feeling too good, it puts me in a state all bloody day and I expect the worst. I get these premonitions but they're twisted. And they're never wrong. I'm in no hurry to come out, Cookie.

Horn   You're nervous and that's normal.

Leonie   You hardly know me!

Horn   Come out, come out then.

Leonie   Are you sure there's only one other man here?

Horn   I'm absolutely positive.

Leonie (*her arm appears*)   I'm parched. When I've had a drink I'll come out, I promise.

Horn   I'll bring you one.

Leonie   Water, just water! I've some pills to take and they're to be taken with water. (**Horn** *leaves;* **Leonie** *appears and looks around.*) It's so impressive. (*She leans over and picks a flower from the bougainvillaea, and then goes back inside.*)

Scene 3

Below the veranda. **Horn** *arrives.*

Cal (*at the table, his head in his hands*)   Toubab, you poor animal, why did you have to go? (*He cries.*) What did I do to him? Horn, you know me, you know my temper. If he doesn't come back tonight, I'll kill them all; dog-eating swine! They've taken him from me. I can't sleep without him, Horn. They're probably eating him now. I don't even hear him barking any more. Toubab!

Horn (*setting up the game of dice*)   Too much whisky. (*He pushes the bottle aside.*)

Cal   Too much silence.

Horn   Fifty francs.

Cal (*lifting his head*)   On five numbers?

Horn   On each.

Cal   Not for me. Ten francs per number, that's as high as I go.

Horn (*suddenly looking at him*)   You've washed and shaved.

Cal   You know I shave every evening.

Horn (*looking at the dice*)   Mine. (*He collects.*)

Cal   Well, I just want to play with chips; for fun, pure fun. You collect and collect, it's not fun any more; all you enjoy is collecting, that's disgusting: every man for himself and nothing for the fun of it all. A woman'll bring a bit of humanity around here. I'm sure it won't be long before she's disgusted with you. Now, I'm in it for the fun, not the money. We should play with chips. Women prefer to play with chips. Women bring humanity to the game.

Horn (*quietly*)   There's a man over there, Cal. He's from the village, or the police, or worse, I've never seen him before. He won't say who sent him here. But you can be

sure he's going to want an explanation and you're going to
have to give it to him. Remember: I'm not getting mixed
up in it; my mind's elsewhere; I don't know anything; I
won't cover for you; I wasn't there. My work is over so
goodbye. This time you'll answer for yourself; and you
can't even take a stinking drop of whisky.

Cal But it's got nothing to do with me, Horn, I didn't
do anything, Horn. (*Quietly.*) Now is not the time to split
up, we have to stick together, we have to stay firm, Horn.
It's simple: you do one report for the police, and one for
the directors, you sign it, and bingo; I'll keep calm. Now
you, everybody believes you; I've only got my dog,
nobody listens to me. We have to stand firm together
against everything. I'm not talking to that nigger; it's all
very simple, I've told you the truth, it's up to you now.
You know what my temper's like, Horn, you know what
I'm like; it's better that I don't see him. Anyway, I don't
want to see anybody until my dog comes back. (*He cries.*)
They're going to eat my dog.

Horn I'll put fifty on each and nothing less.

Cal (*he puts down fifty francs. The croaking of frogs close
by*) We were looking at the sky, me and the workers; the
dog could smell the storm brewing. A lad was crossing the
site; I saw him. At that moment, the storm breaks. I
shout: here Toubab, here! The dog raises his nose and his
fur stands on end; he can smell death and it excites him,
poor bugger. Then I see him running after the nigger,
through all the heavy rain. Come here, Toubab! I call
him, poor bugger. Then in the middle of all this racket,
through the lightning, there's a huge thunderbolt.
Toubab froze; we all saw it. We saw the nigger fall,
through the thunder; hit, under tons of rain; lying in the
mud. There's a faint smell of sulphur; and then, the
sound of a truck coming towards us. (**Horn** *shakes the
dice.*) Toubab's gone, I can't sleep without him, Horn.
(*He cries.*) He's slept on me ever since he was little;
instinct's always brought him back to me. He can't

manage on his own, Horn, poor bugger. I don't hear him barking; they must have eaten him. At night he was like a ball of fur on my tummy, on my legs, on my balls; it helped me sleep, Horn, he's in my blood. What did I ever do to hurt him?

Horn (*looking at the dice*)   Twelve. (**Cal** *collects.*)

Cal (*with a wink*)   Quite a surprise, Horn! You say: I'm going to the airport; you come back and say: my wife's here! I've got to hand it to you. I didn't even know you'd found one. What's got into you all of a sudden, you old dog! (*They place their bets.*)

Horn   A man should put down roots before it's too late.

Cal   Quite right, old man, of course. (*He collects.*) What's important is that you make the right choice.

Horn   So, the last time I was in Paris, I said to myself: If you don't find her now, you never will.

Cal   And you found her! Now that's luck, old man! (*They place their bets.*) Watch the weather though. It does strange things to women. It's been scientifically proved.

Horn   Not to this one. (**Cal** *collects.*)

Cal   She'll need a good pair of shoes, old man, I can lend her a pair. Women want to look elegant, old man, but they're not aware of these African germs, that you get through the feet.

Horn   This is no ordinary woman.

Cal (*winking*)   I'll need to make a good impression on her. I'll find an occasion to kiss her hand, then she'll know what real class is.

Horn   I asked her: do you like fireworks? Yes, she said. Each year in Africa I put on a display, I said, and this will be the last. Would you like to see it? Yes, she said. Then I gave her the address and the plane fare: be there in a month, that's as long as it takes for the package from Ruggieri to get there. Yes, she said. That's how I found

her. I wanted a woman to see the last firework display.
(*He places his bet.*) I told her that they're closing down the
site and that I'm leaving Africa for good. She said yes to
everything. She always says yes.

Cal (*after a pause*)   Why are they closing down the site,
Horn?

Horn   Nobody knows. Here's my fifty. (**Cal** *places his
bet.*)

Cal   Why's it all so sudden, Horn? Why no explanation?
I want to go on working, Horn. And the work that's been
done? Half the forest cut down, twenty-five kilometres of
road? A bridge under construction? And the housing, the
wells we've dug? All that work for nothing! Horn, why
don't we know anything about what's been decided? Why
don't you know?

Horn (*looking at the dice*)   That's mine. (*Silence; the calls
of the guards.*)

Cal (*quietly*)   He's grinding his teeth.

Horn   Who?

Cal   There, behind the tree, the nigger, tell him to go,
Horn. (*Silence. The sound of barking in the distance;* **Cal**
jumps up.) Toubab! I can hear him. He's over by the
sewer; let him fall in, I'm not moving. (*They place their
bets.*) Shit; he's wandering around and won't answer when
I call him, it's like he's thinking about it. Is that him? Yes.
Think about it, you old mutt; I'm not going to fish you
out. He must have picked up the scent of a strange animal;
that's his problem; he won't fall in and if he does, I'm not
moving. (*They look at the dice.* **Cal** *collects; quietly:*) I
hope you don't mind me telling you, Horn, but that lad
wasn't a proper worker, just a hired labourer; no one
knew him, no one will talk about it. He wanted to leave;
and I said no, you're not going anywhere. Leaving the site
an hour early; an hour's an hour; if you let one of them do
it, they'll all want to do it. So as I told you, I said no. So
he spat at my feet and left. He spat at my feet, two

centimetres closer and it would have hit my shoes. (*They place their bets.*) Then I called the other lads together and I told them: you see that guy? (*Imitating an African accent.*) – Yes boss, we see him. – Is he leaving the site without waiting for the whistle? – Yes boss, yes boss, without waiting for the whistle. – Without a hat? Hasn't he got a hard hat? – No, boss, you can see he is not wearing his hard hat. Then I say: remember this: he left without my permission. – Yes boss, oh yes boss, without your permission. Then he fell; the truck arrived and I asked again: who's driving the truck? And why is he going so fast? Didn't he see the nigger? And then, wham. (**Cal** *collects.*)

Horn Everybody saw you shoot him. Idiot, you can't control your bloody temper.

Cal It was like I told you: it wasn't me; he fell.

Horn He was shot. And everybody saw you get into the truck.

Cal The shot was the clap of thunder; and the truck, they were all blinded by the rain.

Horn I may not have had much of an education, but I can see your lies coming a mile off. Well, you'll see what they're worth. Me, I'm off, you're an idiot and it's not my problem. A hundred francs.

Cal I'm in.

Horn (*thumping the table*) Why the hell did you have to touch him? Whoever touches the corpse is responsible for the crime, that's how it is in this bloody country. If nobody had touched it, there would be no responsibility, it would be a crime with no guilty party, an open-and-shut case, an accident. It could have been so simple. But the women came for the body and there was nothing there, nothing. Idiot. They didn't find anything. Try getting out of this one. (*He shakes the dice.*)

Cal When I saw him, I said to myself: I'm not going to

be able to leave this one in peace. Instinct, Horn, temper.
I didn't even know him; but he spat two centimetres away
from my shoes; but that's the way instinct works: I'm not
going to be able to leave you in peace now, that's what I
said when I saw him lying there. So I put him in the
truck, went as far as the dump and threw him up on top:
that's what you deserve, so there; and then I came home.
But I went back, Horn; I couldn't sit still, I was going
crazy. I hauled him off the dump and back onto the truck;
I took him to the lake and threw him in. But it really
bothered me, leaving him there in peace in the lake. So
back I went, waded into the water up to my waist and
fished him out. He was in my truck, Horn, and I didn't
know what to do: I'll never be able to leave you alone, not
ever, this is stronger than I am. I look at him and say to
myself: This nig-nog's going to turn me into a nervous
wreck. Then it came to me: the sewer, that's the answer;
you'll never go after him in there. And that's how it was,
Horn: to leave him in peace, in spite of myself, once and
for all, Horn; at last I was able to calm down. (*They look
at the dice.*) If I'd have buried him, Horn, then I would
have dug him up. I know what I'm like; and if they'd have
taken him to the village, I would have gone to find him.
The sewer, it was so simple, Horn, it was the best
solution. Besides, it's calmed me down a little. (**Horn** *gets
up;* **Cal** *collects.*) Niggers, old man, the germs on them,
now they're the worst of all; tell her that too. Women are
never really prepared for danger.

Scene 4

Horn (*rejoining* **Alboury** *under the tree*)   I've just found
out he wasn't wearing his hard hat. I was telling you how
careless workers can be; well, I was right. No hard hat:
that clears us of all responsibility.

Alboury   Hard hat or not, let me have the body, Mr
Horn, let me have him as he is.

Horn Look, I'm here to tell you this: it's up to you. Either come out or clear off, but don't lurk in the shadows, behind the tree. It's exasperating to know that someone's out there. If you want to join us at the table, come, I never said you couldn't. But if you don't, please go; I'll see you tomorrow and we'll go over it all at the office. In fact, I'd rather you went. I never refused you a glass of whisky, that's not what I said. So what'll it be? Are you refusing to join me for a drink? Would you prefer to come to the office tomorrow morning? Come on. Choose.

Alboury I am waiting here for the body, that's all I want; and I say: when I have the body of my brother, I will go.

Horn The body, the body! He wasn't wearing a hard hat, your body; there are witnesses; he walked across the site without his hard hat. They won't get a penny, tell them that.

Alboury I will tell them that when I take back the body: no hard hat, not a penny.

Horn Have a bit of thought for my wife. All this noise, these cries in the shadows; it's so frightening here for someone who's just arrived. Tomorrow she'll be used to it, but tonight! Just arrived, and on top of that, she can see, she suspects that there's someone hiding behind the tree. You don't realise. She'll be terrified. Do you want to terrify my wife?

Alboury No, I do not want that; I want to return the body to the family.

Horn Tell them this: I'll give the family a donation of a hundred and fifty dollars. There'll be a further two hundred in it for you; you'll get the money tomorrow. It's a lot. But he's probably the last worker who'll die on this site; and what the hell! There it is. Push off!

Alboury I will tell them that: one hundred and fifty dollars; and I will take the body back with me.

Horn   Tell them, yes, you tell them; that's what they care about. A hundred and fifty dollars will shut them up. They don't care about the rest. The body, ha! The body!

Alboury   I care about it.

Horn   Push off.

Alboury   I will remain.

Horn   I'll have you thrown out.

Alboury   I won't leave.

Horn   But you'll frighten my wife.

Alboury   Your wife will not be frightened of me.

Horn   Yes she will; a shadow, someone there! In the end I'll have to get the guards to shoot you, that's the answer.

Alboury   If you kill a scorpion it always returns.

Horn   Now you're getting angry; what are you saying? Until now, I've always got on well with . . . Am I losing my temper? You must admit you're being downright difficult; you leave no room for negotiation. Make an effort. Stay, OK, stay, if that's what you want. (*Softly*.) I know how angry the people from the council must be, but you have to understand, I have no say in the decisions that come down from on high; a site manager doesn't make decisions; I'm not responsible. Besides, it's time they understood: the government issues orders, orders, but never coughs up; it's been months since they paid us. The firm can't keep sites going when the government doesn't pay up; d'you understand? I know it's not good enough: half-finished bridges, roads that go nowhere. But what can I do, eh? Money, money, money, where does it all go? The country's rich, so why's the treasury empty? I'm not saying all this to annoy you, but how can you explain it?

Alboury   They say that the government buildings have become dens of iniquity; they say that champagne and costly women are flown over from France; that they drink and fuck, day and night, in the ministerial offices, and that's why the treasury is empty, that is what I have been told, sir.

Horn   They fuck, do they! (*He laughs.*) Listen to him laughing at his own government ministers. You know, I like you. I don't like civil servants and you certainly don't look like one. (*Softly.*) So, if things are as bad as you say they are, how long till the young begin to rebel? With all the progressive ideas they pick up in Europe, when are they going to decide to overthrow this rotten régime, take the country in hand, and create some order? Will we ever see the day when roads and bridges get completed? Enlighten me, give me some hope.

Alboury   People also say that when they come back from Europe they bring a deadly passion for cars, sir; and that that's all they can think of; that they play with their cars night and day; that they expect to die in them; and that they've forgotten everything else; that's what I am told they bring back from Europe.

Horn   Cars, even Mercedes, yes; you see them every day, driving like maniacs; what a shame. (*He laughs.*) You don't have any illusions, even about the young, I really like you. I'm sure we're going to get along.

Alboury   I am just waiting to be given back the body of my brother; that is why I am here.

Horn   OK then, explain. Why is it so important to get him back? What's his name? Remind me.

Alboury   Nouofia, that was his known name; he also had a secret name.

Horn   But why his body, what's so important about his body? It's the first time I've seen anything like it; and I thought I understood Africans, life or death means nothing to them. You may be an exception; it's not love, is it, making you so stubborn? Only Europeans go on about love.

Alboury   No, it's not love.

Horn   I knew it, I knew it. I've often noticed that lack of feeling. Of course it shocks many Europeans, although, personally, I don't condemn it; Asians are even worse. But then, why be so stubborn over such a small matter, eh? I've said I'll provide compensation.

Alboury   Often the little people want a small thing, something very simple; but that is what they really want; nothing will make them change their minds; and they would die for it; and even if someone were to kill them, they would still want it, even in death.

Horn   Who was he, Alboury, and who are you?

Alboury   A long time ago I said to my brother: I feel cold; he said to me: that's because there is a little cloud in between you and the sun; I said to him: how can that little cloud make me so cold, when all around me people are sweating and getting burned by the sun? My brother said to me: I too am cold; so we kept each other warm. Then I said to my brother: when will this cloud vanish, so that the sun may warm us once again? He said to me: it will never vanish, it is a little cloud that will follow us wherever we go, always in between us and the sun. And I felt it follow us everywhere, so that in the midst of people laughing, naked in the heat, my brother and I were still cold and still warmed one another. So, beneath this little cloud which deprived us of warmth, my brother and I grew used to each other, and used to sharing our warmth. If my back had an itch, my brother was there to scratch it, and when his back itched I scratched it; worry made me bite the nails on his hands and, in his sleep, he sucked my thumb. Our women stayed close to us and they too began to freeze, but we all kept warm because we remained close to one another under our little cloud, we became used to each other and if one of us shivered it spread from one side of the group to the other. Our mothers came to join us, and the mothers of their mothers and their children and our children, a countless family whose members were never torn away, not even the dead, but retained in our close embrace, sheltered from the cold under the cloud. The little cloud had risen closer and closer towards the sun, depriving the whole family of warmth as we grew ever larger and ever more used to each other, an innumerable family made up of the dead, the living and the unborn, each one ever more indispensable to the other, as we saw the edge of the sun-warmed lands moving away from us. That is why I have come for the body of my brother who has been torn from among us, because his absence has disturbed that closeness which allowed us all to keep warm, because, even though he is dead, we still have need of his heat to warm us and he needs ours if he is to remain warm.

Horn It's difficult for us to understand each other. (*They look at one another.*) However hard we try, I think we will always find it hard to live together. (*Silence.*)

Alboury I have been told that, in America, the black people go out in the morning and the white people go out in the afternoon.

Horn Is that what you were told?

Alboury If it's true, sir, it's a very good idea.

Horn Do you really think that?

Alboury Yes.

Horn No, it's a very bad idea. On the contrary, Mr Alboury, we have to work together, Mr Alboury, we have to force people to cooperate. That's what I think. Look here, my good man, this will leave you speechless. I have an excellent plan of my own, and I've never said a word about it to anyone before. You're the first. You must let me know what you think of it. It's about those three billion people they're always on about: I have worked out that if we housed them all in forty-storey blocks – there are some architectural details to sort out, but it won't need more than forty storeys, not even as tall as the Montparnasse tower – and in average-sized flats, I've allowed for a reasonable living space; and we imagine these blocks making up a town, one town with streets ten metres wide, which is fine. Well, imagine: this town would cover just half of France, not one square kilometre more. Everywhere else would be free, completely free. You can check the figures, I've gone over them again and again, they're quite precise. Do you think my plan sounds stupid? All that remains is to choose the site for this unique town; and then the whole thing is solved. No more wars, no more rich countries and poor countries, everyone in the same boat and plenty for all. You see, Alboury, I'm something of a Communist, in my own way. (*A pause.*) France seems ideal to me: it's a temperate country with good rainfall and no extremes in its climate, its flora and fauna, or the risks to health; yes, France is ideal. You could build it in the south, of course, where it's sunniest. On the other hand, I myself love the winter, a good old hard winter; here you don't know what a good old hard winter is. It would be best to build the town lengthways, running from the Vosges to the Pyrenees and bordering the Alps; people who love the winter would live in the part that used to be Strasbourg while those who can't stand the snow, bronchitics and the like, they could live in the parts where Marseilles and Bayonne used to stand. The last conflict facing humanity would be a theoretical debate between the charms of an Alsatian winter or of spring on the Côte d'Azur. As for the rest of the world, it would all be kept in reserve. Africa could be free, think of it; we could exploit her riches, her minerals, her land, solar energy, without treading on anyone's toes. Africa alone would provide enough food for my town for generations before we would ever need to venture into Asia or America. Technology would be greatly exploited, so that we could make do with the minimum workforce, in well-organised shifts, as a sort of community service; they would bring back oil, gold, uranium, coffee, bananas, whatever you like, without the Africans suffering foreign invasion, because they won't be there any more! France would be beautiful, with all the nations of the world mingling in her streets; and Africa too would be lovely, empty, generous, without suffering, nurturing the world! (*A pause.*) Does my plan make you laugh? At least it's friendlier than yours. Anyway, that's my idea and I'm sticking to it.

They look at one another; the wind intensifies.

Scene 5

Below the veranda.

Cal (*seeing* **Leonie**, *he shouts*)   Horn! (*He drinks.*)

Leonie (*holding her flower*)   What are these flowers called?

Cal   Horn!

Leonie   Do you know where I could get a drink?

Cal   Horn! (*He drinks.*) What the fuck's he doing?

Leonie   Don't call him, don't put yourself out; I can find it myself. (*She moves away.*)

Cal (*stopping her*)   D'you intend to walk around out here in those shoes?

Leonie   My shoes?

Cal   Sit down. What's wrong? Do I frighten you?

Leonie   No. (*Silence; in the distance a dog barks.*)

Cal   In Paris they don't understand shoes; in Paris they know nothing and their fashions are rubbish.

Leonie   Now you tell me; they were all I bought. The crooks, and the price they charged for those little pieces of leather! It was the Saint Laurent Africa boutique, no less. What a price! Madness.

Cal   They should come up higher, and support your ankle. With a good pair of shoes you can survive anything, that's the most important thing, a good pair of shoes. (*He drinks.*)

Leonie Yes.

Cal If it's sweat you're afraid of, that's silly; one layer of sweat dries, and then another and another, and it forms a sort of protective shell. And then if you're worried about the smell, smell develops your instincts. Besides, you get to know people by their smell; it has its practical application, you can pick out what belongs to who, it's very simple, just a matter of instinct.

Leonie Oh yes. (*Silence.*)

Cal Have a glass, why aren't you drinking?

Leonie Whisky? I can't. My tablets. Anyway, I'm not thirsty.

Cal Thirsty or not, here you have to drink. If you don't, you get dehydrated. (*He drinks; silence.*)

Leonie I've a button to sew on. That's me all over; but I can't do buttonholes, they're too hard for me. No patience, none at all. I always leave them till last and then end up with a safety pin. I've made the nicest dresses, but I swear I always end up fastening them with a safety pin. Flirt, one day you'll prick yourself.

Cal I used to be like that with whisky, couldn't stand it; and I used to drink milk, nothing but milk, I can tell you; litres, churns of the stuff; before I travelled. But since I started travelling, there you go: disgusting powdered milk, American rubbish, soya milk, none of which has ever been near a cow. So, I had to turn to this shit. (*He drinks.*)

Leonie Yes.

Cal Luckily you can find this shit everywhere; there's no corner of the world where I haven't found it. And I've done a lot of travelling, believe you me. Have you travelled?

Leonie Oh no, this is my first time.

Cal I may look young but I've done some travelling,
believe me, believe me. Bangkok, been there, Isfahan, the
Black Sea; Marrakesh, been there, Tangiers, La Réunion,
Caribbean, Honolulu, Vancouver too; Chicoutimi; Brazil,
Colombia, Patagonia, Majorca, Minorca, Guatemala, yes;
and finally this shit pit Africa, now, Dakar, Abidjan,
Lomé, Leopoldville, Johannesburg, Lagos; it's worse
than anywhere, Africa, let me tell you. Well everywhere, I
found whisky and soya milk; no problem. I'm still young,
you know; well, let me tell you, one whisky tastes like any
other, one site's like any other, one French firm just like
any other; all the same old shit.

Leonie Yes.

Cal No, this firm isn't the worst, don't go making me
say what I don't mean. It might actually be the best. It
knows how to look after you, treat you right, good food,
good quarters, a good French firm; you'll see; you won't
hear me say a word against it, remember that. (*He drinks.*)
It's not like those shit firms run by the Italians, the
Dutch, the Germans, the Swiss and I don't know how
many more, who are all crowding into Africa, turning it
into a right dump. No, ours isn't like that; it's a good firm.
(*He drinks.*) I wouldn't want to be Italian or Swiss,
believe you me.

Leonie Oh yes oh no.

Cal Drink that. (*He hands her a glass of whisky.*)

Leonie Where on earth can he be? (*Silence.*)

Cal (*softly*) Why did you come here?

Leonie (*startled*) Why? I wanted to see Africa.

Cal See what? (*A pause.*) This isn't Africa. It's a French
construction site, doll.

Leonie All the same . . .

Cal No. You interested in Horn?

Leonie   We're getting married, yes.

Cal   You're marrying Horn?

Leonie   Yes, yes, Horn.

Cal   No.

Leonie   Why do you keep saying . . . Where is Cookie?

Cal   Cookie? (*He drinks.*) Horn can't get married, you know that, don't you? (*Silence.*) He did tell you . . .

Leonie   Yes, yes, he told me.

Cal   So he told everything?

Leonie   Yes, yes, yes.

Cal   He's a brave guy, Horn. (*He drinks.*) He spent a whole month alone, here, with a few nig-nogs, all alone; guarding the equipment during their shitty little war; they wouldn't have got me to do that. So he told you everything, his scrap with the looters, his wound – a terrible wound, poor Horn – everything? (*He drinks.*) He's a born gambler, Horn.

Leonie   Yes.

Cal   No. Where's it got him? What's left for him, do you know that?

Leonie   No, I don't know that.

Cal (*with a wink*)   But at least you know what's missing! (*He drinks.*) Something strange about this business. (*He looks at her.*) What is it about you that interests him? (*Calls of the guards; silence.*)

Leonie   I'm too thirsty.

She gets up, and walks off amongst the trees.

Scene 6

The wind whips up red dust; **Leonie** *sees someone beneath the bougainvillaea.*

*In the whispers and flurries, in the beating of wings which
surround her, she recognises her name, and then she feels the
pain of tribal scarification marks on her cheeks.*
*The harmattan, sandy wind, carries her to the foot of the
tree.*

Leonie (*approaching* **Alboury**)   I'm looking for water.
Wasser, bitte. (*She laughs.*) Do you understand German?
It's the only foreign language I know a bit of. You see, my
mother was German, pure German, born and bred; and
my father was from Alsace; so with all that . . . (*She
approaches the tree.*) They must be looking for me. (*She
looks at* **Alboury**.) But he told me . . . (*Gently.*) Dich
erkenne ich, sicher. (*She looks all round.*) When I saw the
flowers I recognised everything; I recognised these
flowers though I don't know their name; but they were
hanging from the branches like that in my mind, and all
the colours, I already had them in mind. Do you believe
in reincarnation? (*She looks at him.*) Why did he tell me
there was no one here but them? (*Agitated.*) I believe in it,
I do. Happy times, blissful times which come back to me
from far away; so gentle. This must be very old. Or so I
believe. There's a lake I know, I've spent a whole lifetime
on its banks, and it comes to me all of a sudden, in my
mind. (*Showing him a bougainvillaea flower.*) You only
find these in hot countries, don't you? But I recognised
them coming from far away, and now I'm looking for the
rest, the warm waters of the lake, the blissful times. (*More
agitated.*) I was already buried once under a yellow stone,
somewhere, beneath flowers like these. (*She leans towards
him.*) He told me there was no one. (*She laughs.*) And
there's you! (*She moves away.*) It's going to rain, isn't it?
So tell me, how do insects manage when it rains? One
drop of rain on their wings and they perish. So what
happens to them, in the rain? (*She laughs.*) I am so glad
that you aren't French or anything like that; it means you
won't think I'm an airhead. Besides, I'm not really
French either. Half German, half Alsatian. You see, we're
made for . . . I'll learn your African language, and when I

can speak it well, really choosing my words, then I'll tell
you . . . things . . . important things . . . which . . . I
don't yet know. I daren't look at you, you're so serious,
and me, when people are serious! (*She moves restlessly.*)
Can you feel the wind? When it circles round like that it's
the devil circling you. Verschwinde, Teufel; pschtt, go
away. They used to ring the cathedral bells to drive out
the devil when I was a child. Is there no cathedral here?
It's funny to think of a country without cathedrals; I like
cathedrals. And you're standing there, so serious; I like
serious people. (*She laughs.*) I'm a little flirt, sorry. (*She
stops moving.*) I would rather stay here; it's so warm. (*She
touches him without looking at him.*) Komm mit mir,
Wasser holen. I'm such an airhead. They must be looking
for me; I'm not supposed to be here, I know that much.
(*She lets him go.*) There's someone there. I heard . . .
(*Softly.*) Teufel! Verschwinde, pschtt! (*Whispering in his
ear.*) I'll come back. Wait for me. (**Alboury** *disappears
beneath the trees.*) Oder Sie, kommen Sie zurück!

Enter **Cal**.

Scene 7

Cal (*a finger to his lips*)   Don't talk too loud, doll; he'd be
unhappy.

Leonie   Who? We're alone here.

Cal   That's right, doll, that's right, we're alone. (*He
laughs.*) Horn's the jealous type. (*Barking, nearby.*)
Toubab? What's he doing here, close by? (*Taking* **Leonie**
by the arm.) Was someone here?

Leonie   Who is Toubab?

Cal   My dog. He barks when he sees a nig-nog. Did you
see someone?

Leonie   You trained him to do that?

Cal   Trained him? I never trained my dog. Pure

instinct, nothing more. But you, look out for yourself if
you see anything. Let the animals fight it out amongst
themselves; run for safety.

Leonie   What? If I see what?

Cal   Knifed in the belly or stabbed in the back, that's
what you'll get if you stop to ask questions and don't run.
I'm telling you: if you see anything at all, anything you've
not seen before, or anything I haven't shown you, then
run quickly and come here for safety. (*Taking* **Leonie** *in
his arms.*) Poor doll! One day, I too arrived here, full of
ideas about Africa; the things you think you'll see, or
hear! In my imagination, I loved it, but what you hear,
and see, isn't what you expect; I know why you're sad.

Leonie   I'm not sad. I was looking for a drink, that's all.

Cal   Your name?

Leonie   Leonie.

Cal   Is it the money you're after?

Leonie   What money? What are you going on about?
(**Cal** *lets her go and approaches the truck.*)

Cal   This woman's a dangerous schemer. (*He laughs.*)
What was your job in Paris?

Leonie   I worked in a hotel. Chambermaid.

Cal   Skivvy. We don't earn as much as you may think
out here.

Leonie   I don't think anything.

Cal   We work hard and earn nothing.

Leonie   Yes you do, I know you earn a packet.

Cal   Where d'you get that from, little skivvy? Do I look
like someone who earns a packet? (*He shows her his hands.*)
Do I look like a man who doesn't work for his living?

Leonie   Just because you work, it doesn't mean you
don't have money.

Cal   Serious money wouldn't wreck your hands, that's
what it means to have serious money. Money overcomes
everything, everything that's hard, no more effort, no
more sweat, no need even to move if you don't want to; no
more pain. That's what money provides. But not us! Get
that out of your head. OK, so they pay us, but not
enough, not nearly enough. Rich people say goodbye to
suffering. (*Looking at* **Leonie**.) With that incident, during
the war, Horn, with that . . . accident, he must have got
heaps of money, old Horn; he never mentions it, so, it
must be loads. Money interests you, eh, doll?

Leonie   Don't call me doll. You're full of words like
that: doll, nig-nog, and the name of your dog. Don't go
giving people dogs' names. No, I didn't follow Cookie for
the money.

Cal   So, why, then?

Leonie   Because he proposed to me.

Cal   You would have followed anyone who proposed to
you, eh? (*He laughs.*) This woman has passion.

Leonie   It wasn't anyone who proposed.

Cal   And you've got a thing about fireworks, eh, doll?

Leonie   Yes, that too, he told me about that too.

Cal   You're a dreamer, eh? And you're trying to put me
in a dream too, eh? (*Harshly.*) But my dreams are real, I
don't dream lies. (*He looks at her.*) This woman is a thief.
(**Leonie** *starts;* **Cal** *draws her back into his arms.*) I'm just
having fun, doll, don't worry. You see, we haven't seen a
woman for so long, I just wanted to have some fun with a
woman. You think I'm a savage, don't you?

Leonie   No, oh . . .

Cal   All the same, we could get savage, if we let
ourselves go. But just because we're in this hole, that's no
reason to let yourself go, that's what I say. Take me, for
instance, I've got loads of interests, you'll see, and I love

to talk, I love having fun, and most of all, I love exchanging ideas. Listen, I was mad about philosophy, I really was. But, what the hell, who gives a damn about that here? No, Africa isn't what you imagine, doll. And then the old guys who are here don't want us bringing in any new ideas; what with the firm and the work, we don't have time. That was my strong point, ideas; I had so many ideas. But when you think, think, think, all alone, the ideas just explode in your head, one by one; as soon as I get one going: bang, like a balloon: bang; as you drove here, you must have seen dogs, on the roadsides, with their bellies all swollen like balloons, and their paws in the air. Now what really matters is exchanging ideas with someone. I've always had an inquiring mind; music, philosophy; Troyat, Zola, especially Miller, Henry Miller. You can come to my room and borrow books, I've got all of Miller, my books are yours. Your name?

Leonie   Leonie.

Cal   As a student, I was really crazy about philosophy. Especially Miller, Henry Miller; reading Miller really blew me away. I went crazy in Paris. Paris, the world capital for great ideas! Miller, yes. When he has that dream that he's shooting Sheldon and saying: 'I'm not a Polack!' You know that bit?

Leonie   I don't . . . No.

Cal   So, when I got out here, there was no question of letting myself go, not me, doll.

Leonie   Leonie.

Cal   This woman is edgy with me. (*He laughs.*) There's no need, you must be absolutely straight. There's nothing standing between us, we're the same age, we're very alike; in any case, I'm being absolutely straight. There's no reason to get uptight.

Leonie   No, there's no reason.

Cal   Anyway, we have no choice: we're alone; you won't

find anyone here to talk to; it's the back of beyond.
Especially now that everything's closing: only me and him
left. And him, when it comes to culture . . . in any case,
he's an old man, Horn.

Leonie An old man! You do say some things! I like
talking to him.

Cal Yes, perhaps not; but sooner or later you need
someone to look up to. It's important, what you look up
to. Women look up to men. What's your name?

Leonie Leonie, Leonie.

Cal So?

Leonie So what?

Cal Why Horn?

Leonie Why what?

Cal You'd marry a man who's not got . . . the full block
and tackle? You'd do that for money? This woman makes
me puke!

Leonie Let me go.

Cal Come on, doll; I only wanted to see your reaction.
As for me, well, it's none of my business. Are you crying
or what? Don't take it like that. I understand why you're
sad, doll. But look at me, am I sad? And I've every reason
in the world to be sad, real reasons. (*Gently.*) I'll lend you
my shoes; it wouldn't do for you to catch some filthy
disease. Here we're all practically savages; I know; this is
the arsehole of the world. But that's no reason to cry.
Look at me: I've studied, I've got degrees, I'm far more
qualified than Horn, and I'm still beneath him. D'you
think that's right? Everything's twisted here. But look at
me, doll, am I making a big crisis out of it? D'you see me
crying?

Leonie Here's Cookie. (*She gets up.*)

Cal Don't move. There's a thief in the camp. It's
dangerous.

Leonie You see thieves everywhere.

Cal It's a nigger. The guards let him in by mistake. You barely see them and you're done for: knifed in the belly, or stabbed in the back! Get into the truck.

Leonie No. (*She pushes him away.*)

Cal I was only trying to protect you. (*After a pause.*) You think I'm a bad lot, doll, I know. But we haven't laid eyes on a woman here, not since the site opened; so seeing one, seeing you, wound me up, that's all. You can't understand that, coming from Paris. But it wound me up, seeing you; I'd much rather be different, because I felt at once that we could be friends. But the way I am, is never the way I want to be. All the same, I'm sure we could get on. I have an instinct, as far as women are concerned. (*He takes her hand.*)

Leonie I'm blushing, oh!

Cal You've got passion, and it shows. I like that, passion. We're alike, doll. (*He laughs.*) This woman is really attractive.

Leonie The women here must be so beautiful. And oh, I feel so ugly! (*She gets up.*) Cookie's here.

Cal (*coming close to her*) Don't be such a cock-teaser, my little skivvy. I've a good instinct when it comes to certain things.

Leonie (*looking at him*) We look so ugly! It's him, I can hear him; he's come to look for me. (**Cal** *holds her very firmly; she manages to escape.*)

Cal Cock-teaser!

Leonie Crook!

Cal Paris, the biggest brothel on earth!

Leonie (*from far off*) Verschwinde, verschwind!

Cal Bitch. (*After a pause.*) When you haven't seen a woman for ages, you expect . . . you imagine some sort of

. . . explosion. And then there's nothing, nothing at all.
Another wasted evening. (*He moves away.*)

Scene 8

At the table with the game of dice.

Horn   Balance, that's the word. Like with food: the
right proportion of proteins and vitamins; the right
proportion of fats and calories; the whole meal should be
balanced as you progress from starters to the main dishes,
then on to the desserts. And that's how a good firework
display is designed, with a sense of balance: a harmonious
progression through the colours, the right proportion of
noise as one explosion follows another, the right
calculation for the height each one should reach. Creating
the overall balance and the balance for each separate
moment, I tell you, that's a real headache. But you'll see,
Cal, you'll see what we've created up in that sky, Ruggieri
and me!

Cal (*suddenly stops playing*)   This game's stupid.

Horn   Stupid? What's so stupid about it?

Cal   I just think it's stupid.

Horn   Good God, I can't see why you think that.

Cal   That's just it, there's nothing to think.

Horn   God, so what more do you want? There's only
two of us, I don't see what else we can play. Maybe you
don't think it's difficult enough for you. We could make it
more difficult, you know, there are variations: we could
set up a bank and say you're only allowed to bet on . . .

Cal   The more difficult it is, the more stupid it is.

Horn   So you give up?

Cal   I give up; it's a game that makes you soft in the
head.

Horn (*after a pause*)   God, I just don't understand.

Cal (*dropping his head into his hands*)   Flop!

Horn   What?

Cal   I tell you, every time we play it's like a lobotomy; (*He strikes his head.*) I can feel it there.

Horn   But what's got into you? In every camp I've been in, everyone plays, and I've never yet seen someone stop mid-game saying: it's like a lobotomy. What's a lobotomy got to do with it? You've never said anything like that yourself, and I've seen you playing all these months . . . If you like I'll get the deck and we can play . . .

Cal   No, no, no; not poker, no!

Horn   Because cards don't . . .

Cal   They're even more stupid.

Horn   So everybody who plays cards is stupid? For centuries people all over the world have been playing cards, they're all stupid and no one's ever realised till now except you? Christ!

Cal   No, no, no, no more games.

Horn   So what are we going to do?

Cal   I don't know. Try not to be stupid.

Horn   All right then. (*They sulk.*)

Cal (*after a pause*)   That's the real sound of Africa. Not the tom-tom, or the pounding of grain, none of that. It's the fan, there, above the table; and the sound of cards or a dice shaker. (*After another pause, very softly.*) Amsterdam, London, Vienna, Crakow . . .

Horn   What?

Cal   All those towns in the North, which I'd love to get to know . . . (*After a pause, they pour themselves another drink.*) I'm putting five hundred on the ten.

Horn   With a bank or without?

Cal   No, the easiest way.

Horn   I'm in. (*They shake the dice.* **Horn** *pushes the whisky bottle to one side.*) You drink too much.

Cal   Too much? Can't be too much. I'm never ever drunk.

Horn   But what's she up to, God, where is she?

Cal   How should I know? (*He collects.*) On the contrary, drunks have always disgusted me. Besides, that's why I like it here. It's always made me sick to be around a drunk. You know, that's why I'd like my next works project to be . . . (*They lay their bets.*) I could have ended up with someone who was pissed every night, it's like that on some sites; I know it is; I could have. (*The dice are shaken.*) You could ask to have me with you on your next project. You carry enough weight, boss; you've got enough seniority in the firm. They'll listen to you, boss.

Horn   There won't be a next project for me.

Cal   Yes there will, boss, you know very well; you know very well, boss. Can you really see yourself in some little house, in the South of France, between your weepy wife and a little garden, boss? You'll never leave Africa. (*He collects.*) It's in your blood. (*After a pause.*) I don't mean to flatter you; but you see, leadership comes naturally, that's in your blood too; you're the kind of boss people get attached to, that's evident, people get used to your being in charge; that's how you know a good boss. I'm used to you, you're my regular boss, no doubt about it, I'm not even aware of it. At the site, when they say to me: boss this, boss that, I always say excuse me, I'm not the boss, Horn's the boss. What am I? Nothing. I am: nothing, I'm not ashamed to say it. Without you: nothing at all. Nothing frightens you; even the law doesn't frighten you. Me, it's the opposite, without you there, well . . . I'm frightened, I'm not ashamed to say it. Frightened, really frightened; faced with a nigger cop, I run; that's the way it is; faced with a nigger who's not a cop, I shoot. It's all

down to my nerves, when you're frightened, there's
nothing you can do about it. Even faced with a woman I'd
panic, boss, that's what I'm like. So you see I need you.
(*Softly*.) Everything's falling apart here; the site isn't
what it was; people come and go at will; so, on top of all
that, if we split up, we'll be all alone. (*More softly*.) Didn't
you act like a prize prick, bringing a woman out here?
(*More softly still*.) What about the nig-nog, d'you think he
came just because he knew there was a woman here?
(*They lay bets*.) We should stick together, hand-in-glove,
that's what I think. Just the thought of ending up in
another camp, with guys who get pissed every night, I tell
you I'd just shoot the lot of them, that's what I'd do.
(*They look at the dice.* **Cal** *collects*.)

Horn (*getting up*) God, what's she doing?

Cal One more game, boss, the last one. (*Smiling*.) A
thousand on the ten. (*He stakes the money;* **Horn**
hesitates.) A born gambler like you, boss, surely you're
not hesitating? (**Horn** *places the stake; they shake the dice*.)
Wait. (*They listen*.) He's talking.

Horn Behind the tree. He's still there and he's talking.

*They listen. The wind suddenly drops; the leaves sway and
then stop; the dull sound of bare feet running over stone in
the distance; leaves and cobwebs fall; silence.*

Scene 9

Alboury *crouching beneath the bougainvillaea. Enter*
Leonie*; she crouches down opposite* **Alboury***, at a
distance.*

Alboury Man naa la wax dara?

Leonie Wer reitet so spät durch Nacht und Wind . . .

Alboury Walla niu noppi tè xoolan tè rekk.

Leonie Es ist der Vater mit seinem Kind. (*She laughs*.)

You see, I can speak foreign too! We'll manage to understand each other in the end, I'm sure we will.

Alboury   Yow dégguloo sama lakk waandé man dégg naa sa bos.

Leonie   Yes, go on speaking like that, you'll see, I'll get it eventually. And can you understand me? If I speak very slowly? You shouldn't be frightened of foreign languages, quite the opposite; I've always thought that if you look at people very carefully, for a long time, while they're talking, you can understand them. You just need to take your time. I speak foreign, and you too, so we'll soon be on the same wave-length.

Alboury   Wax ngama dellusil, maa ngi nii.

Leonie   But slowly, OK? Or we'll get nowhere.

Alboury (*after a pause.*)   Dégguloo ay yuxu jigéén?

Leonie   Siehst, Vater, du den Erlkönig nicht?

Alboury   Man dé dégg naa ay jooyu jigéén.

Leonie   Den Erlenkönig mit Kron und Schweif?

Alboury   Yu ngelaw li di andi fii.

Leonie   Mein Sohn, es ist ein Nebelstreif. It's coming, isn't it? You see. Oh, of course, the grammar takes time, we'll have had to spend a lot of time together before it's perfect; but even with mistakes . . . What counts is a little vocabulary; not even that, it's the tone of voice that's important. In fact you don't even need that, all you need to do is to look at each other, without speaking. (*Pause; they look at each other; the barking of a dog in the distance; she laughs.*) No, I can't do it, we'll be silent when we understand one another. Right now I'm lost for words. I'm usually such a talker. But when I look at you . . . You impress me; but I like being impressed. Now, please, it's your turn to say something.

Alboury   Yow laay gis waandé si sama bir xalaat,

bènbèn jigéén laay gis budi jooy te di teré waa dëkk bi nelaw.

Leonie   Again, but slower.

Alboury   Jooy yaa ngimay tanxal.

Leonie (*softly*)   You're the only man here who looks at me when I speak.

Alboury   Dégguloo jooyu jigéén jooju?

Leonie   Yes, yes, I wonder why I came at all. They all frighten me now. (*She smiles at him.*) Except you. And I still know nothing of your language, nothing, nothing. (*In a deep silence two guards call to one another, sharply, brutally; then the silence returns.*) It doesn't matter, I'd like to stay with you longer. I feel so terribly foreign.

Alboury   Lan nga ñäw ut si fii?

Leonie   I think I'm beginning to understand you.

Alboury   Lan nga ñäw def si fii?

Leonie   Oh, I knew it would come!

Alboury (*with a smile*)   Are you frightened?

Leonie   No.

Suddenly a whirlwind of red sand, bringing with it the cries of a dog, flattens the grass and bends the branches, while from the ground there rise, like an upwards rain, clouds of maddened, suicidal mayflies, veiling the light.

Scene 10

At the table.

Cal   Another evening wasted, a whole evening spent waiting around; isn't it a funny evening? We keep dropping the game and picking it up again, we wait for the woman, then she disappears, and then there's the fireworks. But for the moment, look at the only fireworks we're going to get out of Africa: a cloud of dead bugs.

Horn (*examining an insect*)   Strange: it hasn't rained yet, they usually come out after the rain. I'll never understand this stinking country.

Cal   What a waste, that's what you call a real waste: the woman can't even be bothered with you: she's probably off in some corner weeping or whatever. Of course, it doesn't surprise me; as soon as I saw her I had a feeling. I'm not trying to upset you, boss, not at all. Your money's your own, it's yours to buy whatever pleasures you want, boss. But never think you can count on women for pleasure in life; they're fucked, women are; we men can't rely on anyone but ourselves; you've just got to tell them: we get pleasure, more pleasure out of a job well done – you can't deny it, boss! – now that's solid pleasure and no woman can beat it: a solid bridge built with our hands and our heads, a good straight road that can stand up to the rains, that's where real pleasure lies. Women, boss, they'll never understand what men get pleasure from, now don't deny it, boss, I know you can't.

Horn   I don't know, maybe, maybe you're right. I remember the first bridge I built; the first night, after we'd got the last girder in place, all the finishing touches done, the night before the big opening, here's what I remember: I stripped off and I wanted to lie down and sleep there naked, through the night, on that bridge. I nearly died a dozen times that night, I was all over the damned bridge, touching it everywhere, hauling myself up the cables and then catching sight of the whole thing, white beneath the moon, rising out of the mud, and I remember so well how white it was.

Cal   But you're leaving this one half finished; it's a waste.

Horn   It's not up to me.

Cal   I should've stuck with my first idea and gone into the oil business, yeah, that's what I dreamed of. There's something classy about oil. Look at the guys who work the rigs, the way they look down on us: they know damned well they're top dogs. Me, I've always been fascinated by oil; everything that comes from under the ground fascinates me. Bridges, now they disgust me; look at us, public works projects, what are we? Compared to the oilmen, we're nothing, misery itself, less than nothing. We just work on the surface, like idiots, in front of the whole world, with an unskilled workforce. What sort of man works here? Men who heave, shove, lift, drive; mule-men, elephant-men, beasts of burden; we're all beasts of burden, we're a dumping ground for men with no qualifications. It's not like oil: there, with just six or seven qualified men, look, boss, you have a fortune running through your hands! I'm just a beast of burden too, that's what I've come to. I've got qualifications, they're here, they're here! But I need to be stretched. When I look over there, at night, and I see the flares on the oil fields, I just stare for hours.

Horn (*placing a bet*) Play.

Cal I'm not up to it, boss, no, my heart's not in it. (*Softly.*) So, you're really going to drop me, Horn, is that what's on your mind? Say it, say it: you're going to drop me, aren't you, boss?

Horn What?

Cal Tell the guards to shoot. Shit, it's our right!

Horn Don't worry about that. Just play and stop worrying.

Cal Why d'you speak to him? What did you say? Why the fuck don't you have him thrown out?

Horn That one, he's not like the others.

Cal I knew it; you're being had; I'd really like to know what you were saying; in any case, you're dropping me, I can see that.

Horn   Idiot; don't you see I'm going to fuck him over, that's all there is to it.

Cal   You're going to fuck him over?

Horn   I'm going to fuck him over.

Cal   All the same, you're acting strange with that nigger.

Horn   Christ, who's in charge here?

Cal   You are, boss, I never said you weren't. But that's just it . . .

Horn   Who has to go round cleaning up everyone else's mess? Who has to organise every last little detail, from one end of the camp to the other, and then from dawn to dusk at the building site? Who has to keep everything in his head, from the smallest spare part on one of the trucks to the number of whisky bottles left in the store? Who has to deal with the planning, the estimates, the ordering, night and day? Who has to be cop, mayor, boss, general, head of the family, ship's captain?

Cal   You, boss, you, no question.

Horn   And who's had it up to here, right up to here?

Cal   You, boss.

Horn   That's right; I may not have qualifications, but I'm still the boss, it's still me.

Cal   I'm not trying to wind you up, boss, I just wanted to let you know, in passing, that you seemed to me to be acting strange with that nigger, Horn, talking to him normally, that seemed strange, that's all. But if you say you'll finish the job, then you'll do it.

Horn   It's all taken care of.

Cal (*after a pause*)   You're still a strange guy. Let me take care of him, it'll be so much quicker.

Horn   You'll do nothing. Leave it to me.

Cal   You have strange ways of doing things.

Horn Christ, you can't just shoot your way through life. Look at me: I've got a tongue in my head, I've learned to speak and to use words. Maybe I didn't go to school, but I can talk. You just blast your way out of trouble and then go crying to someone else to drag you out of the mess. Is it just shooting they teach you in those fancy engineering schools, nothing about learning to reason? That's just great! Well, do it your way; go round shooting at everything and then come crying back to me, just come crying. This is the last time for me, after this I'm off. And when I'm gone, you can do what you like.

Cal Don't get shirty, boss.

Horn You just destroy everything, that's all any of you learn to do in your fancy schools. Well carry on, gentlemen, fuck the whole place up. You could've helped them to like you, instead all of Africa hates you. And in the end you'll have achieved absolutely nothing. All of you, you're all mouth, trigger-happy and out for a quick buck at any price, well I tell you, gentlemen, the lot of you: in the end you'll have nothing, nothing and nothing again. Africa, you couldn't care less about Africa, could you? All you think about is grabbing as much as you can and giving nothing back, above all, give nothing back. Well, you'll end up with nothing at all, and that's all there is to it. And the Africa we knew will be utterly destroyed, you bastards.

Cal Me, I'm not destroying anything, Horn.

Horn You don't love Africa.

Cal Of course I love her, of course I do. Would I be here if I didn't?

Horn Play.

Cal My heart's not in it, boss. It's the risk, sitting here, in the middle of the camp, knowing that some nig-nog can get you in the back, it fucks up my nerves, boss. If you ask me, he's here to take advantage of the situation and stir up a riot. That's how I see it.

Horn   You don't see anything. He's just trying to impress us. That's politics.

Cal   Or maybe it's because of the woman, like I said before.

Horn   No, he's got something else on his mind.

Cal   On his mind, what mind, a nig-nog's mind? You're dropping me Horn, I see it.

Horn   How can I drop you, idiot?

Cal   So will you prove it was an accident, Horn, will you prove it?

Horn   An accident, yes, why not? Who said it wasn't?

Cal   I knew it. We have to stick together; together we can really get them. Now I see it: the talking was to give you time to fuck him over; there's a method in it, I don't say there isn't. But watch out all the same, boss. With all your method, you may still end up with a bullet in the gut.

Horn   He's not armed.

Cal   Never mind, never mind, never mind, you should still watch out. They all do karate, those bastards, and they're strong with it. They can have you on your back before you can say a word.

Horn (*showing him two bottles of whisky*)   I'm armed. No one can resist the whisky . . .

Cal (*looking at the bottles*)   Beer would've been good enough.

Horn   Play.

Cal (*places a bet with a sigh*)   What a waste!

Horn   But while I'm talking with him, you find the body. Don't argue, do whatever's necessary but get the body back. I have to have it. Otherwise the whole village will be on my back. Find it by dawn, or I'll drop you good and proper.

Cal No, it's impossible, no. I'll never find it. I can't.

Horn Find another one, any one will do.

Cal But how, how am I supposed to do that?

Horn He can't be far off.

Horn No! Horn.

Horn (*looking at the dice*) I win.

Cal Your methods are shit. (*He thumps his fist on the game.*) You're a shit, a real shit.

Horn (*getting up*) Do what I say. Or I drop you. (*He goes out.*)

Cal That bastard's dropping me. I'm fucked.

Scene 11

On the site, at the foot of the unfinished bridge, in the half-dark, **Alboury** *and* **Leonie**.

Leonie You've wonderful hair.

Alboury They say our hair is wiry and black because the father of all blacks, abandoned by God and then by humanity, found himself alone with the devil, who had also been abandoned, so the devil caressed his head as a sign of friendship, and that is how our hair was burnt.

Leonie I love stories about the devil. I love the way you tell them; your lips are wonderful; besides black is my best colour.

Alboury It's a good colour to hide in.

Leonie Listen, what's that?

Alboury The song of the buffalo toads: they are calling for rain.

Leonie And that?

Alboury   The cry of the hawks. (*After a pause.*) There is also the sound of an engine.

Leonie   I can't hear it.

Alboury   I hear it.

Leonie   It's the sound of water, it's the sound of something else; with all these sounds, it's impossible to be sure.

Alboury (*after a pause*)   Did you hear?

Leonie   No.

Alboury   A dog.

Leonie   I don't think so. (*Barking of a dog in the distance.*) It's a little puppy, it's not a real dog at all, you can tell by its bark; it's a pooch, miles away; now you can't even hear it.

Alboury   It's after me.

Leonie   Let it come. Me, I love dogs, I stroke them, they don't attack you if you love them.

Alboury   They're evil beasts; me, they can smell me from miles away, they hunt me down and bite me.

Leonie   Are you frightened?

Alboury   Yes, I'm frightened.

Leonie   Of a silly little puppy which you can't even hear any more!

Alboury   We frighten chickens; dogs frighten us; that's normal.

Leonie   I want to stay with you. What's left for me with them? I've given up my job, I've given up everything; I've left Paris oiyoiyoiyoiy, I've left everything behind. I was looking for someone to be faithful to. I found him. Now I'm staying put. (*She shuts her eyes.*) I think there's a devil in my heart, Alboury; I don't know how he got in but he's there, I can feel him. He's caressing my soul so that I'm burning, all black on the inside.

Alboury   Women speak so fast; I can't keep up.

Leonie   Fast, you call that fast? When I've been thinking of nothing else for the last hour, thinking about it for an hour and I'm not allowed to say it's serious, that I've considered it carefully, that it's final? Tell me what you thought when you saw me.

Alboury   I thought: there's a coin lost in the sand; for the moment nobody sees it shining; I can pick it up and keep it till someone claims it back.

Leonie   Keep it, nobody's going to claim it back.

Alboury   The old man said you belonged to him.

Leonie   Cookie? Are you worried about Cookie? My God, he wouldn't hurt a fly, poor Cookie. What d'you think I am to him? A little company, a passing whim, because he's got money and doesn't know what to do with it. And as I'm broke, wasn't I lucky to meet him? Aren't I a cunning little flirt? If my mother knew, she'd be furious, she'd have said: you slut, luck like that only comes to actresses or whores; all the same, I'm neither one nor the other and it came to me. And when he asked me to join him in Africa, yes I said yes, I'm ready. Du bist der Teufel selbst, Schelmin! Cookie's so old, so sweet; he never asks for anything, you know. That's why I like old men, and on the whole they like me too. Often they smile at me in the street, I feel good with them, I feel close to them, I like their vibes; d'you feel the vibes from old men, Alboury? Sometimes I can't wait to be old and sweet myself; to be able to talk for hours, not expecting anything from anyone, not being afraid of anything, not saying bad things about people, leaving cruelty and unhappiness behind, Alboury, oh why are men so hard? (*Light cracking of a branch.*) How calm it all is, how gentle! (*Cracking of branches, confused calls in the distance.*) You and me here, it's so good.

Alboury   For you, yes; but for me, no. This is a white man's place.

Leonie   Stay a little, just one minute more. My feet hurt. Those shoes are awful; they cut into your ankle and your toes. Look, can't you see the blood? Look at this rubbish: three little pieces of leather stitched together any-old-how, just the thing to tear your feet and for this rubbish you pay the earth. Oh, I just can't face walking in them for miles.

Alboury   I will have kept you for as long as I could. (*Sound of truck approaching.*)

Leonie   It's coming.

Alboury   It's the white man.

Leonie   He won't hurt you.

Alboury   He will kill me.

Leonie   No!

They hide; the van is heard, stopping; the ground is lit up by the headlights.

Scene 12

Cal, *a rifle in his hand, covered with blackish mud.*

Horn (*emerging from the darkness*)   Cal!

Cal   Boss? (*He laughs, runs towards him.*) Ah, boss, am I glad to see you.

Horn (*pulling a face*)   Where have you crawled out from?

Cal   Out of the shit, boss.

Horn   God, don't get any closer, you'll make me throw up.

Cal   You're the one, boss, you told me to do whatever I had to to find him.

Horn   Well? Did you?

Cal Nothing, boss, nothing. (*He weeps.*)

Horn So you covered yourself with shit for nothing! (*He laughs.*) God, what an idiot!

Cal Don't make fun of me, boss. It was your idea, and I'm always left to sort things out on my own. It was your idea, and because of you I'll go down with tetanus.

Horn Get inside. You're completely drunk.

Cal No, boss, I want to find him, I must find him.

Horn Find him? You're too late, you idiot. He's far away by now, drifting down who knows what river. And the rain's coming. Too late. (*He goes towards the van.*) The seats must be in one hell of a state. God what a stench!

Cal (*grabbing him by the collar*) You're the one in charge, you're the big white chief. You tell me what to do. You can't let go now. I can't swim and I'm drowning, old man. Besides, I'm warning you, you jerk, nobody laughs at me.

Horn Watch out, you're losing control, don't get so wound up. Cal, come on, you know I wouldn't laugh at you, not at all. (**Cal** *lets him go.*) So what happened? We should disinfect you right away.

Cal Look how I'm sweating, bloody hell, look at that, it won't dry off. You got a beer? (*He weeps.*) You wouldn't have a glass of milk? I want a drink of milk, old man.

Horn Calm down; we'll go back to the camp; you'd better clean yourself up. It's going to rain.

Cal So can I shoot him now, can I shoot him?

Horn God, don't talk so loud.

Cal Horn!

Horn What?

Cal Am I a bastard, old man?

Horn   What are you talking about? (**Cal** *weeps*.) Cal, my boy.

Cal   I suddenly saw Toubab, standing in front of me, looking at me with his little pensive eyes. Toubab, my little dog! I said: what are you dreaming of, what's on your mind? He growls and his fur stands on end as he slowly moves along the sewer's edge. I follow him. Toubab, my little dog, what are you thinking? Did you smell someone? His fur stands on end, he gives a little bark, and he jumps into the sewer. So I think: he smelt someone. I follow him. But I found nothing, boss; nothing but shit, boss. All the same, that's where I threw him in, but he must have slipped away. I can't follow every water-course in the region and drag the lake to find the corpse, boss. And now Toubab has slipped away as well. I'm all alone again and I'm covered in shit. Horn!

Horn   What?

Cal   Why am I being punished, old man? What have I done that's so wrong?

Horn   You did what you had to do.

Cal   So can I shoot him, boss, is that what I have to do now?

Horn   God, don't shout like that, d'you want to be heard all the way to the village?

Cal (*loading his rifle*)   This little spot is perfect: no one can see you, no one can make demands or come crying. Here you can disappear into the ferns, you bastard, here your skin isn't worth a dollar. Now I'm back to my old self, I feel hot, old man. (*He begins to sniff around.*)

Horn   Give me that gun. (*He tries to grab it from him;* **Cal** *resists.*)

Cal   Watch your step, old man. I may not be much good at karate, I may not be up to much with a knife but I'm deadly with a gun. Deadly, deadly. Even with a revolver or a machine gun, you don't stand a chance.

Horn Do you want the whole village on our backs? Do you want to have to explain yourself to the police? Are you determined to go on playing the fool? (*Softly.*) Do you trust me? Do you trust me or not? Then leave it to me. Don't let your temper get the better of you, my boy. You have to stay calm if you want to sort things out, and before dawn everything will be sorted, believe me. (*A pause.*) I can't stand blood, my boy, not at all; I've never been able to get used to it, never, it drives me crazy. I'll speak with him again, one more time, and this time I'll have him, believe me. I have a few secrets up my sleeve. What would be the point of these years spent in Africa, if I didn't know them better than you, know them like the back of my hand, and if I didn't have my own ways and means which they are helpless against, eh? Where's the point in bloodshed, if things can be sorted out without it?

Cal (*sniffing*) Scent of a woman, scent of a nigger, scent of ferns crying out. He's there, boss, can't you smell him?

Horn Stop trying to be clever.

Cal Can't you hear it, boss? (*Distant barks.*) Is that him? Yes, it's him; Toubab! Come here, my little dog, come, and don't ever go away again, come and be stroked, my little darling, come and be kissed, you little mutt. (*He weeps.*) I love him, Horn; Horn, why am I being punished, why am I a bastard?

Horn You're not a bastard!

Cal But you're a jerk, a fucking jerk, boss. Of course I am, of course I'm a bastard. What's more, I want to be one, it's my choice. Me, I'm a man of action; you, you're a talker, you talk, all you can do is talk; and what will you do if he won't listen, eh? If all your little secret ways and means don't work, eh? Hell, of course they won't work, and then it'll be a good thing I'm a bastard, a good thing there are bastards, to do something about it. Fucking jerks can't take action. If a nig-nog spits at me, I gun him

down and I'm bloody well right to; and it's thanks to me
that they don't spit on you, not because of all your talk,
your jerk-talk. If he spits, I shoot, and that suits you fine:
because two centimetres nearer and it would have been
our shoes, ten centimetres higher our trousers, and a bit
higher still it would have hit us in the face. What would
you do then if I stood by? Would you carry on talking
with his spit dripping down your face? Fucking jerk.
They spit all the time round here and what do you do
about it? You pretend not to see it. They open one eye
and spit, open the other and spit, spit as they walk, eat
and drink, sitting down, lying down, squatting down;
between each mouthful, between each gulp, every minute
of the day; in the end it covers the sand on the site and all
the tracks, it seeps inside and turns into mud, and when
we walk on it our lousy boots just sink in. Now what
exactly is spit made of? Who knows? Liquid, of course,
like the human body, ninety per cent liquid. But what
else? Ten per cent of what? Who can tell me? You?
Nigger-spit is a threat to everyone. If we gathered up all
the spit from all the niggers of all the tribes in the whole
of Africa on one single day, digging pits, canals, dykes,
locks, dams, aqueducts; if we gathered together in streams
all the spit spewed out by the black race all over the
continent, spewed out against us, we could cover every
country on the planet with a sea of menace; and there
would be nothing left except oceans of salt water and
oceans of spit, all mixed up, and only the niggers would
survive, swimming in their element. I'm not going to let
that happen; I'm in favour of action, I'm a man. So when
you've finished all your talking, old man, when you've
finished, Horn . . .

Horn   Let me try first. If I can't convince him . . .

Cal   Ah ha, boss.

Horn   But calm down first. Get your girlie hysterics
under control, for God's sake.

Cal   Ah ha, boss.

Horn   Look, Cal, my boy . . .

Cal   Shut it. (*Distant barking;* **Cal** *is off like an arrow.*)

Horn   Cal! Come back, that's an order: come back!

Sound of a truck starting up. **Horn** *remains still.*

Scene 13

Cracking of branches. **Horn** *switches on his torch.*

Alboury (*in the shadow*)   Switch it off!

Horn   Alboury? (*Silence.*) Come on. Show yourself.

Alboury   Switch off the torch.

Horn (*laughs*)   Why are you in such a state? (*Switches off his torch for a moment.*) Your voice, it's quite something: it scares me.

Alboury   Show me what you are hiding behind your back.

Horn   Ah, yes, behind my back! Rifle or revolver? Guess the calibre. (*He brings two bottles of whisky out from behind his back.*) Ah ha. That's what I was hiding. Are you still suspicious of me? (*He laughs, switches on the torch.*) Come now, relax. They're my best bottles; I want you to taste them. Just remember, Mr Alboury, I've made the first moves; you'd do well to remember that when we come to settle up. You won't come to me, so I come to you; and believe me, I'm doing this out of friendship, pure friendship. What else could I do: you've got me worried; well, interested. (*He holds up the whisky.*) This will loosen you up a bit. I've forgotten the glasses: I hope you're not snobbish; besides, whisky tastes better from a bottle, it stops evaporation; that's how you recognise a real drinker; I'd like to teach you to drink. (*Softly.*) Is there something troubling you, Mr Alboury?

Alboury   Why?

Horn   I don't know. You keep looking over your shoulder.

Alboury   The other white man is after me. He has a gun.

Horn   I know, I know, I know; why do you think I'm here? He won't try anything while I'm around. Here, I hope you don't mind sharing, straight from the bottle? (**Alboury** *drinks*.) Cheers, at least you're not snobbish. (**Horn** *drinks*.) Just give it time to go down; it takes a little time to reveal its secret. (*They drink*.) So, I hear you were a karate champion; were you really that good?

Alboury   It depends on what you mean by good.

Horn   You're not giving anything away! But I'd really like to learn one or two moves, if we get the time, some day. I should warn you right away that I'm not one for the martial arts. Good old-fashioned boxing! Have you ever gone in for good old traditional-style boxing?

Alboury   No, not traditional style.

Horn   But how can you expect to defend yourself then? I'll show you a punch or two one of these days. I was really good, I even fought as a professional when I was young; and it's an art you never forget. (*Softly*.) Calm down; don't worry; you're my guest, and as far as I'm concerned, hospitality's a sacred duty; besides, you're almost on French soil here; there's no need to be afraid. (*They move from one bottle to the next*.) I really want to know which of these you prefer; it says a lot about a man's character. (*They drink*.) This one is sharp, genuinely sharp; can you feel the sharpness? Whereas the other is clean and smooth, it rolls down like thousands of tiny ball-bearings, don't you think? How does it seem to you? Ah, there's no doubt about the sharpness of this one; if you let it go down slowly you get a prickly sensation, a little tingle in your mouth, don't you? Well?

Alboury   I feel no ball-bearings, no sharpness, no prickles.

Horn No? But they're definitely there. Try again. Unless you're afraid you'll get drunk?

Alboury I shall stop before that.

Horn Good, very good, excellent, bravo.

Alboury Why did you come over here?

Horn To see you.

Alboury Why did you want to see me?

Horn To look at you, to chat, to pass the time. Out of friendship, pure friendship. For a whole lot of other reasons too. Do I bore you? Didn't you say you had a lot to learn?

Alboury I have nothing to learn from you.

Horn Bravo, very true, I had a feeling you were laughing at me.

Alboury The one thing I have learned from you, in spite of you, is that there is not enough room in your head or in all your pockets to hide all your lies; in the end they all come tumbling out.

Horn Bravo; but now that's simply not true. Try me; ask me anything, I can prove I'm not lying to you.

Alboury Give me a gun.

Horn Anything but that; you're all going mad with these popguns.

Alboury He's got one.

Horn So much the worse for him. Forget that idiot. He'll end up behind bars and it's no better than he deserves. I'd be happy if someone just got him off my back. I might as well come clean, Alboury, he's the cause of all my troubles; get him off my back and I won't lift a finger. You might as well come clean with me too, Alboury: what do your bosses want?

Alboury I have no bosses.

Horn So why make out you're from the secret police?

Alboury Doomi xaraam!

Horn OK, if you prefer, we can go on playing hide-and-seek. It's up to you. (**Alboury** *spits on the ground*.) There's no need to get angry.

Alboury How could a man find his way through all your deceit and lies?

Horn Alboury, I'm telling you straight: do what you want, I won't cover for him any more; it's not a lie, believe me. I'm not deceiving you.

Alboury It's a betrayal.

Horn Betrayal? Betrayal of what? What are you saying?

Alboury Of your brother.

Horn Ah no, please, spare me the African jargon. What that man does is not my business, his life means nothing to me.

Alboury But you are of the same race, are you not? Speak the same language, belong to the same tribe?

Horn The same tribe, I suppose so, yes.

Alboury You are both bosses here, are you not? You both decide if the construction site opens or closes, and face no accountability. You hire and fire. You stop and start the machines. You both own the trucks and the machinery, the brick huts and the electricity, everything here, both of you, don't you?

Horn OK, all right, if you want, that's more or less it. So what?

Alboury Why are you so afraid of the word brother?

Horn Because, Alboury, in the past twenty years the world has changed. Look at him and you can see what's changed: it's the difference between us, between a rapacious, homicidal maniac, who's out of control, and a man who came here in a totally different spirit.

Alboury I know nothing of your spirit.

Horn Alboury, I've been a labourer too. Believe me,
I'm not a boss by nature. When I came here, I knew what
it meant to be a labourer and that's why I've always
treated my workforce, white or black, indiscriminately,
the same way I was treated. That's the spirit I'm talking
about: the knowledge that if you treat a worker like a beast
he'll turn on you like a beast. That's the difference. Now,
as for the rest, you're not going to blame me for the fact
that the workers are unhappy, here, or anywhere else;
that's just the way it is, I can't do a damn thing to change
that. I'm paid to know that. D'you think there's a worker
anywhere in the world who can say: I'm happy? D'you
really think there's a single human being in the world who
can say: I'm happy?

Alboury What do the feelings of the bosses matter to
the workers, or the feelings of the whites to the blacks?

Horn You're a hard man, Alboury, I can see that. As far
as you're concerned, I'm just not human; it doesn't matter
what I say, what gesture I make, what ideas I have, even if
I pour out my heart to you, all you see in me is a white
man and a boss. (*After a pause.*) What the hell. It doesn't
stop us drinking together. (*They drink.*) It's strange. I feel
you're never quite there, as if there was someone behind
you; you're so distracted! No, no don't say anything, I
don't want to know. Drink. Are you drunk yet?

Alboury No.

Horn Very good, bravo. (*Softly.*) I've got a favour to
ask you, Alboury. Don't say anything to her, don't tell her
what brings you here, don't talk about corpses or other
disgusting things, don't try to influence her, don't say
anything that'll make her run away. I hope it's not too
late. Perhaps I shouldn't have brought her here, I know, I
just got it into my head, that's how it was. I know it's
madness but it was driving me crazy, and now, no, don't
frighten her. I need her; I need to feel that she's around

the place. I hardly know her, I don't even know what
turns her on, I just leave her be. It's enough to have her
around, that's all I ask. Don't frighten her off. (*He
laughs.*) What d'you expect, Alboury, I don't want to end
up all alone, like an old fool. (*He drinks.*) I've seen lots of
corpses in my life, lots of them, and lots of eyes, corpse's
eyes; now every time I look at the eyes of a corpse I tell
myself: treat yourself to everything you want to see, spend
your money quick. Otherwise, what is there to spend it
on? I have no family. (*They drink.*) Goes down nicely,
doesn't it? Alcohol doesn't seem to frighten you, that's
good. Are you drunk yet? You're a hard man. Show me.
(*He takes his left hand.*) Why do you grow your nail so
long, just that one? (*He examines the nail on* **Alboury**'s
little finger.) Is it something religious? A secret? That
nail's been bothering me for the last hour. (*He touches it.*)
It must be a hell of a weapon, if you can use it, quite a
stiletto. (*Lower.*) Maybe it's a love tool? Ah, my poor
Alboury, if you're not careful, women will ruin you! (*He
looks at him.*) But you just keep silent, you hang on to all
your little secrets; I'm sure that, deep down, you've been
laughing at me all along. (*He suddenly pulls out a bundle of
banknotes from his pocket and holds it out to* **Alboury**.)
There you are, my boy. As promised. Five hundred
dollars. It's the best I can do.

Alboury   You promised me the body of Nouofia.

Horn   The body, yes, hell, the body. You're not going
to start that again, are you? Nouofia, that's right. And he
had a secret name, you said. What was it again?

Alboury   It's the same for all of us.

Horn   That's a big help. What was it?

Alboury   I'm telling you: it is the same for all of us.
There is no other way to say it; it is secret.

Horn   You're too deep for me; I like things to be clear.
Come on, take it. (*He holds out the bundle of notes.*)

Alboury   That is not what I want from you.

Horn Now come on, Mister, don't exaggerate. A worker is dead, sure; it's serious, sure, I have no desire to minimise the importance of the thing, not at all. But it happens, everywhere, all the time; d'you think that workers don't die in France? It's terrible, but it happens; it's part of the job; if it hadn't been him it would've been someone else. What d'you think? Work here is dangerous; we all take risks; but they're not excessive, it's always within limits, proportionally speaking. Let's get this straight. Work has a cost and you can't change that. Any society offers up a part of itself. Do you imagine that I've made no sacrifices? It's the way of the world. It doesn't stop the world going round, not even you can stop the world turning, eh? Don't be naive, my good Alboury. Be sad, I can take that, but don't be naive. (*He holds out the money.*) Here, take it.

Enter **Leonie**.

Scene 14

Lightning, more and more frequent.

Horn Leonie, I was looking for you. It's going to rain and you can't imagine what rain is like round here. Give me a minute and then we'll go in. (*To* **Alboury**, *softly*.) You're just too deep for me, Alboury. Your thoughts are all mixed up, dark and impenetrable, like the bush round here, like the whole of Africa. I wonder why I loved it so much; I wonder why I tried so hard to save your skin. It seems as if everyone round here is going mad.

Leonie (*to* **Horn**) Why are you giving him such a hard time? (**Horn** *looks at her*.) Give him what he asked for.

Horn Leonie! (*He laughs.*) Good God, do we have to be so solemn? (*To* **Alboury**.) You'd better know: the workman's body can't be found. It's drifting somewhere, it must have been swallowed up by fish and birds of prey, long ago. Once and for all, will you give up the idea of getting it back. (*To* **Leonie**.) It's going to rain, Leonie, come. (**Leonie** *walks over to* **Alboury**.)

Alboury   Give me a gun.

Horn   God, no. There will be no slaughter here. (*After a pause*.) Let's be reasonable. Leonie, come. Alboury, take the money and get out of here before it's too late.

Alboury   If I have lost Nouofia for ever, then I shall not rest until his murderer is dead.

Horn   Thunder and lightning, man; settle your score with the heavens and push off, out, get out this time! Leonie, come here!

Scene 15

Leonie (*softly*)   Take it, Alboury, take it. He's even offering you money, nicely, offering you money, what more do you want? He came over to sort things out; well then, if possible, things should be sorted out. Why go on fighting for something that no longer has any meaning, when someone's kindly offering to sort it out, with money, as well? That other one, he's just a maniac, but we know that now, all three of us have to be careful, and make sure he doesn't wreck everything, that's it, stop him doing harm, and then everything will go like clockwork. He's not like that at all; he just wanted to talk nicely, but you, you have to say no, you clench your fists, you play stubborn, oh! I've never seen such stubbornness. D'you think that's the way to get what you want? My God, he hasn't even the first idea how to go about it, not the first idea; now, you let me try, I could handle things: and there'd be no clenched fists, no hostility and no stubbornness, oiyoiyoiyoi. I don't want to go to war or fight, I don't want to be left shaking with fear and unhappiness. I just want to live, quietly, in a nice little house, wherever you say, in peace. I don't mind being poor, that doesn't bother me, I'll fetch water and chop branches and do whatever's needed; I'd be quite happy to live on nothing at all, but I don't want killing and fighting and clenched fists, no, why must everything be so hard? Maybe I'm not worth as much as a half-eaten corpse, not even worth that? Alboury, is it because I have the misfortune to be white? But don't get me wrong, Alboury. I'm not really white. I'm so used to being something I shouldn't be that there's no problem in being a nigger on top of everything else. If that's all it is, Alboury, my whiteness, I spit on it, have done for ages, I don't want it. So if you don't want me either . . . (*A pause.*) Oh black, colour of my dreams, colour of my love! I swear it: when you go back home I'll go with you; when you say: my house, I too will say: my house. Your brothers will be my brothers, your mother will be my mother! Your village will be mine, your language will be mine, your earth will be my earth and I'll follow you even into your dreams and beyond death, I swear, I'll still be with you.

Horn (*from a distance*)   You can see he doesn't want you. He's not even listening to you.

Alboury   Démal falé doomu xac bi! (*He spits in* **Leonie**'*s face.*)

Leonie (*turning towards* **Horn**)   Help me, help me.

Horn   What? After you've carried on so shamelessly with him, under my very nose, and you still want me to help you? D'you think you can treat me like shit and I'll just stand there? D'you think you can touch me for cash, just for cash, and then treat me like shit? God, you're going back to Paris, tomorrow, yes. (*Turning towards* **Alboury**.) As for you, I could have you shot like a common tramp. How dare you make yourself at home here, and treat me like shit? You think we're all just shit? It's really lucky for you that I can't stand sodding bloodshed. But I'm warning you, just get off your high horse and show a bit of remorse. Did you really think you could con a French woman under my very nose, on French property, and not have to pay for it? Get out of

here. You can sort things out with the others in the village
when they discover that you've conned a white woman so
as to blackmail us. And I leave you to sort out how to get
away without running into the other guy who's out to skin
you alive. Get out, scram, and if we see you in the camp
again you'll be shot, by the police if needs be, like a
common thief. I wash my hands of your sodding hide.

Alboury *has disappeared. The rain starts to fall.*

Scene 16

Horn   As for you, I beg of you, spare me your tears; that
would be the last straw. No, no, no, I can't stand tears,
crying drives me crazy, stop it, I beg of you, where's your
shame? What on earth gave me this idea in the first place?
I've been such a fool. Stop, stop, stop, please, show some
shame. People will hear, you pick up the smallest sounds
from miles away; we must look a right pair, I swear; if
only you could see what a spectacle you're making of
yourself. Ssh, come on, do whatever you need to pull
yourself together, but ssh! Take a deep breath, do what
you want, drink in one enormous gulp, like you do for
hiccups, perhaps that'll work, but stop it. Here, drink.
(*He throws her the bottle.* **Leonie** *drinks.*) Another, don't
hold back and it'll restore your decency, all this is in such
bad taste. What the hell is Cal doing with his sodding
truck? Cal! Oh God. Please! Don't imagine that lad isn't
still hanging around watching us, ha! gloating at the sight
of your pitiful, shameful scene. What a picture you give of
the white man. God, that was some idea of mine. Leonie,
I beg you, I can't bear scenes. (*He walks up and down,
back and forth.*) I'll feel awful now, yes, really, really
awful. (*He stops suddenly close to* **Leonie**. *Softly and very
fast.*) Please, what if . . . if we cleared off, eh? If I left the
camp straight away, would you . . . (*He takes her hand.*)
Don't . . . stop crying . . . don't leave me alone. I've got
enough money to leave without notice and Cal could take

over, and then in two days we'd be in France or
anywhere, in Switzerland, or in Italy, on the lake of
Bolsena, or Lake Constance, anywhere you like. I've got
the money, plenty of it. Don't cry, don't cry, Leonie, with
you I . . . Say yes. Don't leave me, I feel so awful, Leonie,
I want to marry you, that's what we both wanted, isn't it?
Say yes!

Leonie *has stood up. She breaks the whisky bottle on a stone
and quickly, without a cry, looking at the shadows into which*
Alboury *has vanished, she takes a shard of glass, and cuts
deeply into her cheeks, making scarification marks similar to
the tribal markings on* **Alboury**'s *face.*

Horn   Cal! God, Cal! She's bleeding; it's so senseless.
Cal! There's blood, everywhere!

Leonie *passes out.* **Horn** *runs, screaming, towards the
approaching headlights.*

Scene 17

At the camp, near the table, **Cal** *is cleaning his rifle.*

Cal   I can't do a thing with the lights on. Not a thing.
The guards would see me do it and they might testify
against me. They might run off to the police and I don't
want anything more to do with the police; or they might
run off to the village and I don't want the village on my
back: I can't do a thing with all this light.

Horn   The guards won't make a move. They're too
grateful for the work and they hang on to that, believe me.
Anyway, why would they run off to the police, or to the
village when it would cost them their jobs? They won't
move, they won't see, or hear a thing.

Cal   They've let him in once, haven't they, and again
just now. He's there, behind the tree; I can hear him
breathe. The guards aren't to be trusted.

Horn   They can't have seen him come in, or else they

were asleep. Anyway, you can't hear them now. They're asleep; they won't move.

Cal   Asleep? You're going blind, boss. I can see them. They're facing this way, they're looking at us. Their eyes are half closed but I can see they're not asleep and they're looking at us. Look, one of them just brushed away a mosquito with his arm; that one's scratching his leg; there, one of them just spat on the ground. I can't do a thing with all this light.

Horn   (*after a pause*)   We'd better make sure the generator has some sort of breakdown.

Cal   We'd better, yes; it must. Otherwise, I can't do a thing.

Horn   No, better still, let's wait till morning: then we'll send out a radio call and the van can go to town. Come on, I'm going to set up the mortars.

Cal   The what?

Horn   The rockets, the Roman candles: all the equipment for my fireworks.

Cal   But it's almost day, Horn! Besides, she's shut herself into the bungalow, she won't want to come out and watch the fireworks, she didn't even want any treatment; if she goes down with tetanus, we'll be stuck with her. What a strange woman. Now she'll have those marks for life; and she was quite pretty. Strange. And you . . . Who do you think's going to watch your fireworks, boss?

Horn   Me, I'll watch them; I'm doing it for myself, that's why I bought them.

Cal   And what am I supposed to do? Let's stick together, old man; now we really have to finish the job.

Horn   He's all yours. Just be careful.

Cal   Only thing is, I've cooled down now, I don't really know what I'm doing.

Horn One black skin's just like any other, isn't it? The village wants a body, we'll give them one; there'll be no peace till we've done it. If we wait much longer they'll send in a couple of guys to demand the body, and then we'll be stuck.

Cal But they'll see it's not the worker. They can tell each other apart.

Horn He could be unrecognisable. If you can't make out the face, who can say: it's him, or: it's someone else! The face is all they have to go on.

Cal (*after a pause*) I can't do a thing without the rifle; I don't like close combat and they're too strong, those bastards, with their karate. The trouble with the rifle is that they'll see the hole in the head as evidence and then we'll all have the police on our backs.

Horn So, it's best to wait till morning. Let's do it all by the book, my boy, that's best. We'll talk to the police and sort it out as best we can, by the book.

Cal Horn, Horn, I can hear him there, he's breathing. What can I do? What should I do? I don't know what I'm doing. Don't leave me.

Horn He could be run over by a truck. Who could say: that was a gun shot, or: he was struck by lightning, or: a truck went over him, eh? A gun shot can't be recognised after the victim's been run over.

Cal I'm going to bed after all. My head's killing me.

Horn Idiot.

Cal (*threateningly*) Don't you call me idiot, Horn, don't you ever call me idiot again.

Horn Cal, my boy, calm down! (*After a pause.*) What I mean is that if we let him go back to the village now, two or three of them will be back, and just try sorting things out then, with two or three of them! Whereas, if we get his body taken into the village tomorrow and we say: here's the guy who was struck by lightning yesterday, on the site, he was run over by a truck. Then, everything will sort itself out.

Cal   But then they'll start asking questions about this one; they'll ask: where did this one get to?

Horn   This one isn't a worker, we have nothing to answer for there: never seen him. We know nothing. OK?

Cal   In cold blood, just like that, it's hard.

Horn   When there are several of them and, after that, when the guards let everyone in, what'll we do then, eh?

Cal   I don't know, I don't know; you tell me, old man.

Horn   Better to shoot the fox than lecture the hen.

Cal   Yes, boss.

Horn   Besides, I've softened him up. He's not dangerous any more. He's been drinking like a fish; he can barely stand.

Cal   Yes, boss.

Horn (*softly*)   Take care, hit him full in the face.

Cal   Yes.

Horn   And after that, the truck, carefully.

Cal   Yes.

Horn   Take care, great care.

Cal   Yes, boss, yes boss.

Horn   Cal, my boy, look here, I've made up my mind, I shan't stay till the work's completed.

Cal   Boss!

Horn   Yes, my boy, that's the way it is; I've had it up to here; I don't understand Africa any more; new methods are needed, I suppose, and I don't understand them. So, when you come to close everything down, Cal, for God's sake, listen, don't hide anything from the management, don't try to fudge things, tell them everything, get them on your side. They'll understand it all, they'll be able to sort it all out, the whole bang shooting match. Even the police, don't say a word: let them talk to the firm. The management of your firm, that's the only thing that exists for you, just hang onto that.

Cal Yes, boss.

Horn In two hours the sun'll be up; I'm going to set off the fireworks.

Cal What about the woman, boss?

Horn She'll leave with the van. I don't want her mentioned. She never existed. We're alone. Cheers.

Cal Horn!

Horn What?

Cal There's too much light, much too much light.

Horn *raises his eyes to the surveillance towers and the stationary guards.*

Scene 18

In front of the half-open door of the bungalow.

Horn (*speaking into the bungalow*) In a few hours, a van will be taking some papers into town; the driver'll sound the horn; be ready; you can trust him. In the meantime it might be dangerous to come out; lock yourself into your room and don't move, whatever you do, until you hear the horn. By the time you leave I'll already be at work so I'll say goodbye. See a doctor when you get back. I hope he'll be able to patch you up, yes, perhaps a good doctor could patch you up and make you presentable again. Another thing, when you get back, please don't talk too much. Think what you like, but don't do anything to harm the firm. It gave you hospitality, after all; don't forget that; don't harm it: it's not responsible for what happened to

you. I'm asking you this as . . . as a favour. I've given the
firm everything; it's everything to me, everything. I don't
care what you think of me, but don't harm the firm
because then it would be my fault, yes, all my own fault.
You can grant me this one favour; after all it's my money
that's paid for the ticket that's taking you home; you
accepted the ticket out, now you must accept the ticket
home. So, there we are . . . Bye-bye. I won't see you
again; we won't meet again. Ever. (*He exits.*)

Leonie *appears, on the doorstep, carrying her cases. Her
face is still bleeding. Suddenly, the lights go out for a few
seconds, then the generator can be heard starting up again.*

Cal *appears;* **Leonie** *hides her face behind her hands and
stays in this position for as long as* **Cal** *looks at her.*

Scene 19

The lights still flicker from time to time, interrupting **Cal**.

Cal   Don't worry, don't worry, doll, it's the generator.
Those big machines are tricky to handle; looks like it's
going to break down, it happens, Horn must be trying to
sort it out, don't worry. (*He moves towards her.*) I washed.
(*He sniffs.*) I don't think I smell any more. I put on some
after-shave. Do I still smell? (*A pause.*) Poor doll; it won't
be easy to get another job now, I should think, eh;
especially in Paris; hell. (*A pause.*) It's probably snowing
in Paris now, what d'you think? You're quite right to go
back; in any case I knew; I always knew he'd end up
disgusting you. I still can't understand what you saw in
him. When I first saw you from a distance, getting off the
plane, red, all red! And with your Parisian elegance, so
chic, so up to date, but so fragile! And to look at you now
. . . Horn, what a jerk! Cellars and sewers aren't for kids;
he should have known that. Kids should be left to play on
the terrace, in the garden, cellars should be forbidden. All
the same, you know, you brought a glimpse of humanity
to us who work out here. Perhaps I do understand Horn

after all, the old dreamer! (*He takes her hand.*) In any case
I'm really pleased to have met you, doll, I'm glad you
came. I'm not fooling myself, doll, I'm sure you have a
bad opinion of me. But it doesn't matter what you think
as you're going back to Paris, and we'll never see each
other again. I'm sure you'll bad-mouth me to your girl-
friends for a while and I know that you'll have bad
memories of me, and in the end you won't remember me
at all. But that doesn't mean I didn't enjoy exchanging
ideas with you. (*He kisses her hand.*) When will we see
your like again, doll, a real woman like you? When will we
have fun with a woman again? When will I ever see a
woman again in this god-forsaken hole? I'm wasting my
life here; I'm wasting what, anywhere else, would be my
best years. When you're alone, always alone, you even
forget how old you are; but seeing you, I remembered.
Now I must forget again. And what does my existence
here amount to? Nothing. All that just for money, baby;
money drains you of everything, even the memory of how
old you are. Look. (*He shows her his hands.*) Would you
think these were the hands of a man who's still young? In
the end I wonder why, yes why I'm alive at all. (*The lights
go out, for good this time.*) Don't worry; it's just a
breakdown; don't move. I've got to go; farewell, baby-
doll. (*After a pause.*) Don't forget me, don't forget me.

Scene 20: Last visions of a distant enclosure

*A first shower of light breaks out for a brief moment, silently,
in the sky above the bougainvillaeas.*
*Blue flash from a rifle barrel. Dull sound of bare feet running
over stone. Death rattle of dog. Glimmers from a torch. A
short tune is whistled. Sound of a rifle being loaded. Cool
breath of wind.*
*The horizon is filled with an enormous, multi-coloured sun,
which falls back down, with a muffled sound, scattering
sparks on the camp.*
Suddenly **Alboury**'s *voice is heard: out of the darkness*

arises a call, a secret warrior call, which is carried away by the wind, rising up from the clump of trees to the barbed wire and from the barbed wire to the watchtowers.

Intermittently lit up by the fireworks, accompanied by dull explosions, **Cal** *approaches the stationary silhouette of* **Alboury.** **Cal** *raises his rifle, aiming high, for the head; sweat is running down his forehead and into his eyes; his eyes are bloodshot.*

Then a conversation starts up, in the heart of the dark periods between explosions, an unintelligible dialogue between **Alboury** *and the heights all around. The conversation is tranquil, impassive; brief questions and answers; laughs; an indecipherable language resonating, swelling, eddying along the barbed wire from top to bottom, filling the whole space, governing the darkness and vibrating over the petrified camp, as a final succession of glittering sparks and suns explode.*

Cal *is hit first in the arm; he drops his rifle. Up on one of the watchtowers a guard lowers his gun; on another a second guard raises his.* **Cal** *is hit in the stomach, then in the head; he falls.* **Alboury** *has disappeared. Blackout.*

Day breaks gradually. Cries of hawks in the sky. On the surface of the open sewers empty whisky bottles clink against each other. Sound of a van's horn. The bougainvillaea flowers sway; they all reflect the dawn light.

Leonie (*very far off so that her voice can hardly be heard, obscured by the noises of the dawn; she leans towards the chauffeur*)   Haben Sie eine Sicherheitsnadel? Mein Kleid geht auf. Mein Gott, wenn Sie keine bei sich haben, muss ich ganz nackt. (*She laughs, climbs into the van.*) Stark naked! Nach Paris zurück. (*The van drives off.*)

Beside **Cal**'s *body. On his shattered head is placed the corpse of a white puppy, baring its teeth.* **Horn** *picks up the rifle from the ground, wipes his forehead, and looks up towards the deserted surveillance towers.*

Translations of passages in German and Woloff

Scene 6

Leonie Water, please. [. . .] I'm sure I recognise you.
[. . .] Begone, devil. [. . .] Come with me and get some
water. [. . .] Devil! Begone. [. . .] Or you, come back!

Scene 7

Leonie Begone, begone!

Scene 9

Alboury Can I tell you something?

Leonie 'Who rides so late through night and wind . . .'
[*Translators' note*: Leonie quotes the first lines of
Goethe's poem *Erlkönig*.]

Alboury Or we can keep quiet and look at each other.

Leonie 'It is a father with his child.' [. . .]

Alboury You don't understand my language but I can
understand yours.

[. . .]

Alboury I will repeat what I am saying.

[. . .]

Alboury Didn't you hear screaming nearby?

Leonie 'Father, do you not see the Erlking?'

Alboury I didn't hear screaming nearby.

Leonie 'The Erlking with his crown and train?'

Alboury You were brought here by the wind.

Leonie 'My son, it is a patch of mist.' [. . .]

Alboury   I have seen you but in my own thoughts.
Another screaming nearby, that would prevent the
villagers from sleeping.

[. . .]

Alboury   The screaming is disturbing.

[. . .]

Alboury   Didn't you hear screaming nearby?

[. . .]

Alboury   What have you come here for?

[. . .]

Alboury   What did you come here to do?

Scene 11

Leonie   You're the devil himself, you flirt!

Scene 13

Alboury   Motherfucker!

Scene 15

Alboury   I wouldn't bother with you; I won't give up!

Scene 20

Leonie   Do you have a safety pin? My dress is coming
apart. My God, if you don't have one I shall have to go
stark naked. [. . .] Back to Paris.

Return to the Desert

Le Retour au désert

translated by DAVID BRADBY

Characters

Mathilde Serpenoise
Adrien, *her brother, industrialist*
Mathieu, *Adrien's son*
Fatima, *Mathilde's daughter*
Edouard, *Mathilde's son*
Marie Rozérieulles, *Adrien's first wife, now deceased*
Marthe, *her sister, Adrien's second wife*
Maame Queuleu, *live-in servant*
Aziz, *day-time servant*
The Great Black Parachutist
Saïfi, *café owner*
Plantières, *Prefect of Police*
Borny, *solicitor*
Sablon, *Prefect of the Département*

A provincial town in Eastern France at the beginning of the 1960s

Why grow the branches now the root is wither'd?
Why wither not the leaves that want their sap?

Shakespeare: *Richard III*, II, ii

I: Sobh

Scene 1

Wall running round the garden.
In front of the open door.
Early morning.

Maame Queuleu Aziz, hurry up and come in. We've got a lot of work to get through today; the master's sister is coming back from Algeria with her children. There's so much to prepare, I'll never manage on my own.

Aziz Coming, Maame Queuleu. I thought I heard footsteps and voices, and at this hour of the day, in this street, that seemed strange.

Maame Queuleu The streets are dangerous. Come in quickly. I don't like leaving this door open.

Aziz هَاد النَهَارْ طَالِعْ مَا فِي بَانْش

Enter **Mathilde**.

Mathilde عَلَاشْ غَادِي يكُونْ نْهَارْ خَايِبْ ؟

Aziz إذَا كَانتْ الُأْخْت حُمَارَهْ بْحَالْ خُوهَا ، بَايْنَة ..

Mathilde أنَا عَارْفِتْهَا مِشْ بْحَالْ خُوهَا !

Aziz وكِيفْ تَعْرْفِهَا ؟

Mathilde أنَا هِيَّ خْتُ ...

Enter **Fatima** *and* **Edouard**, *with suitcases.*

Maame Queuleu Come in Aziz, don't hang about outside the door. (*To* **Mathilde**.) Who are you? What are you looking for?

Mathilde Let me through, Maame Queuleu. It's me, Mathilde.

Scene 2

Entrance hall; grand staircase.

Mathilde   Who is this old woman coming down the staircase?

Maame Queuleu   It's Marthe.

Mathilde   Who's Marthe?

Maame Queuleu   Marthe, Marie's sister.

Mathilde   What's she doing here, at this time of day all dressed up like that?

Maame Queuleu   Mathilde, Mathilde, she's Adrien's wife. Have some pity.

*Enter **Adrien**, at the stop of the staircase.*

Adrien   Mathilde, my dear sister, here you are back again in our fine old town. Have you come with good intentions? Now that age has calmed us down, we might make an effort not to squabble during the short period of your stay. I have lost the habit of squabbling during your fifteen-year absence. I should find it hard to resume.

Mathilde   Adrien, my dear brother, I have come with excellent intentions. And I am pleased to hear that age has calmed you down: it will simplify matters during the very long period that I mean to stay here. As for me, age, far from calming me down, has actually stirred me up; so what with your calm and my restlessness everything should turn out fine.

Adrien   You wanted to escape the war and so, naturally, you came back to find your roots here, in this house; you did well. The war will soon be over and soon you will be able to head home to Algeria, to the warmth of the Algerian sun. In the meantime this house will afford you the security you need to survive these troubled times.

Mathilde   My roots? What roots? I'm not a radish; I have feet and they weren't made for being stuck in the ground. And as for the war, my dear Adrien, I don't give a shit. I'm not escaping the war, quite the reverse, I'm going to bring the war home to this fine old town, where I have some scores to settle. The only reason for my taking so long to settle these scores is that too much bad luck had softened me. But fifteen years without bad luck have brought back memories – the faces of my enemies and thirst for revenge.

Adrien   Enemies, my dear sister? Of yours? In our fine old town? Distance must have strengthened your imagination, although it was never exactly weak; and the North African heat must have addled your brains. But if I am right in thinking that you have come to examine your share of the inheritance before moving on, go ahead, examine it, see how well I have cared for it, admire the improvements I have made to the house and then, when you've finished looking, touching, evaluating, we will be glad to see you on your way.

Mathilde   But you are wrong Adrien, my little brother, I do not intend to move on. I have brought my goods and my children. I have come back to this house for the simplest of motives, because it is mine; and with or without improvements, it will always be mine. More than anything else, I want to settle down in what is mine.

Adrien   It is yours, my dear Mathilde, that's right, it is yours. I have paid you rent and I have considerably increased the value of the old pile. But you, of course, are the owner. Don't start making me angry, don't start splitting hairs. I beg you to show me a modicum of goodwill. Why don't we start again from the beginning; we have got off on the wrong foot.

Mathilde   Let's start again then Adrien, let's start again.

Adrien   But don't go thinking, Mathilde my dear sister, that I shall allow you to play the part of mistress of the house and wander round the corridors fiddling with everything. You can't just abandon your field, sit in the shade until some fool comes along to cultivate it and then return at harvest time to claim your crop. The house is yours but it has prospered under me, and, believe me, I shall not relinquish my share lightly. You had the choice. You left the factory to me because you couldn't handle it, and you chose the house because you were lazy. But you abandoned the house to disappear, heaven knows where, and in your absence it has taken on habits of its own; it has its own smells, its own rituals, its own traditions and it knows its own masters. It must not be disturbed, and if you try to turn it upside down I shall protect it.

Mathilde   Why should I want to turn my house upside down when I want to live in it? Judging by its prosperity your factory must be in good shape too. You must have raked in the profits and got into bed with your bankers. Had you been poor, I would have asked you to leave; but since you are rich, I will not send you packing, I will put up with you, your son and the rest of them. But I have no intention of forgetting that the bed in which I shall sleep is my bed, that the table at which I shall eat is my table and that the order or the chaos of the rooms I live in needs no justification beyond my own. In any case, it was time I returned: this house lacks women.

Adrien   Oh no, my dear Mathilde, there is no lack of women, there will always be too many. This house is a house of men; the women who pass through come only as guests and are soon forgotten. It was built by our father and who remembers his wife? I myself have continued his work and who, my poor Mathilde, even remembers your existence? Learn to behave like a guest in your own house; for even if you think you are rediscovering your familiar bed, it is not certain that the bed will recognise you.

Mathilde   But I know for certain that after fifteen years, and ten years more, years and years of sleeping in other beds, I know that I shall go into my room with my eyes closed, that I shall lie down in my bed as if I had always slept there, and my bed will recognise me straight away.

And if by any chance it doesn't, I will shake it until it does.

Adrien   I knew it: you have come here to do evil. You want revenge for your own bad luck. You've deliberately had bad luck so that you could be vindictive; you attract bad luck, you seek it out, you pursue it for the pleasure of being spiteful. You are a dry, hard-hearted woman.

Mathilde   Adrien, you're getting angry. If you have never done me any harm, why should I want to be revenged on you? Adrien, we have still not greeted one another properly. Let's try once more.

Adrien   No, I don't want to try again.

He goes up to **Mathilde**.

Enter **Marthe** *and* **Mathieu**.

Marthe (*to* **Maame Queuleu**)   Who on earth is this woman?

Maame Queuleu   It's Mathilde.

Marthe   Holy Mary, how she's grown.

Adrien   I have forgotten your children's names.

Mathilde   The boy's Edouard, and the girl's Fatima.

Adrien   Fatima? You're mad. We'll have to change that name; we'll have to find her another. Fatima! What on earth will I say when people ask me her name? I don't want to be a laughing-stock.

Mathilde   We shall change nothing at all. A name is not invented, the child picks it up in the cradle, it comes with the air that she breathes. If she had been born in Hong Kong, I would have called her Tsouei Tai, I would have called her Shademia if she had been born at Bamako and if I had given birth to her at Amecameca, her name would be Iztaccihuatl. Who would have stopped me? After all, when a child is born you can't have her stamped for export there and then.

Adrien   At least during your stay, while you're here, at least in front of our friends, let's call her Caroline.

Mathilde   Fatima, come and say hello to your uncle. Edouard, come here.

Marthe   How they have grown! Have they learned to read? Have they read their Bible? The little girl is quite big; does she say her prayers to Our Lady of La Salette? Do they know Mama Rosa, the holy woman?

Mathilde   Adrien, Adrien, are you really married to this?

Adrien   What do you mean?

Mathilde   Her, behind you. You must know what you have married, don't you?

Adrien   Yes, it's true I am married to her.

Mathilde   You are still an ape, Adrien. To marry that after being married to her sister! Marie, poor Marie. Everything that was beautiful and soft and fragile and tender and noble in Marie has been shrivelled up in her.

Adrien   Having her around makes me less guilty about the other one.

Mathilde   What does your son say? Poor Mathieu!

Adrien   My son says nothing. Never mentions it. Not in front of me, in any case. Besides, my son is not poor, he doesn't need your pity.

Mathilde   And you sleep in the same bed? She drinks, doesn't she? I can see it in her face.

Adrien   I don't know. Perhaps. It would seem so. Not in front of me, anyway.

Mathilde   You're more of an arsehole than an ape, Adrien. You prefer the caricature, you prefer the cheap reproduction. You prefer ugliness to everything fine and noble. No, I shall never consider her your wife. Marie is dead, you have no wife.

Adrien   And what about you? You can no more claim to have a husband than I a wife. Where did those two come from? You don't even know yourself. Don't start preaching at me, Mathilde. We are brother and sister, just that. Good morning, Mathilde, my dear sister.

Mathilde   Good morning, Adrien.

Adrien   And there was I thinking you'd come back all brown and wrinkled like an old Arab woman. How do you manage to stay so smooth and white under the infernal Algerian sun?

Mathilde   You take precautions, Adrien, you take precautions. Tell me something, brother, can you still not bear to wear shoes? How do you manage when you have to go out?

Adrien   I don't go out, Mathilde, I don't go out. (*Enter* **Mathieu**.) Maame Queuleu, Aziz, get the bedrooms ready. Mathilde will sleep in her own room with her daughter, and her son will share with mine.

Mathieu   I don't want that boy in my bedroom. I don't want anyone in my bedroom. My bedroom is mine.

Adrien *slaps* **Mathieu**'s *face*.

Edouard   Your bedroom isn't yours, you prat. Come on, Maman, we're moving in.

Scene 3: The secret in the wardrobe

Mathilde's *bedroom.*
A bed and a wardrobe.
Mathilde *is in bed.*
Enter **Fatima**.

Fatima   Maman, I met someone in the garden. Someone I've never seen and who reminded me of someone, a person whose name I dare not say, because that person has forbidden it. Maman, Maman, get up!

Too many strange things are happening in this house and I hate it.

Come with me Maman. The person vanished as soon as a glimmer appeared in the sky, a tiny glimmer, the very first glow of dawn. Come on: I am sure the grass is still trampled and maybe there's a thread of cloth caught on the tree-trunk, where this person leant against it. Maman, this house is full of secrets and it frightens me.

Mathilde   No, I don't want to move. It's taken me hours to warm up these sheets, and now I shan't move again until breakfast time. Come in beside me; it's warm; sleep. We still have hours before they ring the bell for breakfast and already my stomach is groaning. The best thing is to sleep while we wait. You can talk when I've had my coffee.

Fatima   No I can't sleep. This house is evil; it makes me feel dreadful.

Mathilde   You should have seen it in Marie's time! Come under the sheets, come close to me and I will tell you how good Marie was; I will tell you the story of Marie, my friend, my adorable Marie who made this house so warm, so welcoming. I will tell you the story until you fall asleep.

Fatima   Oh you, you think of nothing but sleep and old memories, just when so many things are happening.

Mathilde   How can you say I think of nothing but sleep when I had only just managed to close my eyes after a night of insomnia?

Fatima   You always say that, but the minute you touch the bed you start snoring.

Mathilde   Me, snore? I heard nothing. It's the autumn weather in this town: disgusting dampness and drizzle which blocks up your nose.

Fatima   Maman, Maman, I'm telling you I met someone. Come and see or you won't believe me; the

grass in the garden will have sprung up again and the
wind and the dew will have cleaned the tree-trunk. I want
you to believe me. Get up, put on a dress.

Mathilde   Why must you make such a face, Fatima?
Tell me your secret, tell me; your whole face is swelling
up with it, your eyes are popping; tell me or you'll burst.

Fatima   A secret cannot be told.

Mathilde   I insist you tell me. I know those kinds of
secrets, assignations in the garden at night, and nine
months later there's no secret, just a scandal. Speak to me:
who is this man? What's he done to you? Speak, I insist
you tell me; if you can't tell me, who else can help you
carry the burden?

Fatima   I never said it was a man.

Mathilde   What did you say to him? Did you exchange
words at all? Was it an apparition; could you speak to it?

Fatima   I didn't speak; I was too afraid.

Mathilde   But what it said to you, then, perhaps you
can tell me that? Or was this apparition as dumb as you?

Fatima   No, it spoke to me.

Mathilde   Tell me its name.

Fatima   Never.

Mathilde   Well, go and tell it inside the wardrobe then,
and you'll feel better. Climb in and tell your secret to my
dresses, I don't want to know it. But you'll make yourself
ill if you keep it any longer. (**Fatima** *shuts herself in the
wardrobe and then comes out again.*) Already?

Fatima   It wasn't a long secret.

Mathilde   Well, at least you're not so red any more.
Why make so much fuss for such a tiny secret?

Fatima   I said it wasn't long, I didn't say it was tiny.

Mathilde   I'll put on a dress and go with you. But don't think you can go on living wild over here. Do you think we can go on living like before? (*She opens the cupboard.*)

Fatima   Maman, I didn't ask for this to happen.

Mathilde   Whose name did you speak?

Fatima   No one's, I didn't say a name.

Mathilde   I heard a name.

Fatima   I didn't open my mouth, I just stayed there without saying a thing.

Mathilde   In the folds of my dresses, I heard a name.

Fatima   What would a name be doing in among your dresses? You're dreaming Maman, you're making fun of me. You don't believe me.

Mathilde   Of course I believe you. Let's stay together, let's not separate. I'm frightened now. Come here Fatima, close to me. Let's get down under the sheets.

Fatima   You're shivering Maman, you look cold.

Mathilde   Marie.

Fatima   What? Why did you say that?

Mathilde   Marie, that's the name I heard in the rustling of my dresses.

Scene 4: Mathieu joins up

In the garden.

Adrien (*appearing in front of* **Mathieu**)   Where are you going so early? You haven't had breakfast. Where are you going with that look on your face, as if you were plotting something?

Mathieu   I'm going out.

Adrien   Going out, Mathieu, my son? Out, where from? And where to?

Mathieu   I'm going out of the house, out of the garden, out of everything.

Adrien   And what the hell do you need to go out for? Are you missing something? Aziz can fetch it for you.

Mathieu   I miss going out, and that is something Aziz cannot do for me.

Adrien   Aziz can do everything for you except for one thing and that is to be my son; and I wish to know why my son looks as if he were involved in a plot, so early in the morning.

Mathieu   Why can't I just go out of the house, at my age, without there having to be a plot?

Adrien   You just can't. Do you want to go down to the works? I'll take you in a little while. Do you want to go to church? If you have turned religious you will be taken there after breakfast. Apart from that, where could you go? And where did you get such an idea?

Mathieu   I want to go into town.

Adrien   But you are already in town, Mathieu, my son. Our house is right in the heart of the town. You cannot be more in town than in our house.

Mathieu   I want to take the air.

Adrien   Well then, go and stretch out in the garden, beneath the trees, and I'll have your coffee brought out to you. There is nowhere in the whole town where the air is better than in our garden.

Mathieu   I want to get away.

Adrien   Well then get away, get away, within the limits of the garden. And wipe that suspicious look off your face or at least tell me what's on your mind.

Mathieu   What's on my mind is that I want to leave this house, leave this town, leave this country and join the army.

Adrien   Say that again, Mathieu, my son; this morning my head is troubled by the cries of your aunt.

Mathieu   I want to go and do my military service, go off to Algeria and join the war.

Adrien   Who told you there was a war in Algeria?

Mathieu   I don't what to sleep in the same room as Edouard, I don't want to keep bumping into Edouard all day and all night, I want to go to Algeria because it's the one place where there's no chance of meeting him, since he's just left there.

Adrien   Who told you of the existence of Algeria? You have never been out of here.

Mathieu   I've never been out of here, no; and Edouard makes fun of me because I haven't seen the world.

Adrien   The world is here, my son, you have seen it, you have walked round it every day and there is nothing more to see. Look at my feet, Mathieu: this is the centre of the world; over there is the edge; if you go too near the edge, you'll fall off.

Mathieu   I want to travel.

Adrien   You can travel from your bedroom to the drawing room, from the drawing room to the attic, from the attic to the garden. Mathieu, my son, your mind is disturbed today.

Mathieu   I want to do my military service.

Adrien   They won't take you: you have flat feet.

Mathieu   I do not have flat feet.

Adrien   Who told you that? I have flat feet, therefore you have flat feet too. There are things that a father knows better than his son.

Mathieu   Even if I do have flat feet, I want to be a soldier, I want to parachute into Algeria and make war on the enemy. I want to be a para, Papa, I want to have a military haircut, camouflage uniform, a knife strapped to my leg and a gun in my belt; I want to throw myself out of a plane, I want to float through the air, glide above the ground, singing halfway between the sky and the earth.

Adrien   I must dismiss Aziz and punish Edouard.

Mathieu   I want children to look up to me, I want to be envied by little boys and seduced by women; I want the enemy to be afraid of me. I want to be a hero, risk my life, escape from attacks, be wounded, suffer uncomplainingly, I want to bleed.

Adrien   Be a hero here, where I can see you. Don't you think I've been a hero since your aunt arrived? Don't you think I've always been a hero, bringing you up and making sure you'll inherit the family wealth.

Mathieu   I don't want to inherit the family wealth. I want to die with fine words on my lips.

Adrien   Such as?

Mathieu   I don't know yet.

Adrien   You know nothing. Beyond this wall it's a jungle, and you must never cross it without the protection of your father.

Mathieu   I don't want the protection of my father. I don't want to get my face slapped, I want to be a man who slaps other people's faces; I want mates to drink with and fight with; I want enemies to kill and defeat; I want to go to Algeria.

Adrien   Your enemies are in your own house. Your only mate is your father; if you want to drink, drink; and I won't slap you any more. In any case, there's no such place as Algeria and you will only make yourself look stupid.

Mathieu   Edouard has told me about Algeria.

Adrien   Edouard is a pathological liar, he has disturbed your mind.

Mathieu   I've heard you talking about the war too.

Adrien   The war is over, it has been won, the
countryside is calm, everyone is going back to work.

Mathieu   I want to go to Paris; I don't want to live in
the provinces any more: you always see the same faces and
nothing ever happens.

Adrien   Nothing? You call that nothing? Your aunt and
your cousins descend on us and you call that nothing?
Mathieu, my son, the French countryside is the only
place in the world where life is good. The whole world
envies us our countryside, its peace and quiet, its little
villages, its mellowness, its wines, its prosperity. There is
nothing left to be desired in the country here; you have
everything a man could desire. Or else your mind must be
disturbed, if you prefer poverty to riches, hunger and
thirst to a full stomach, fear and danger to security. Is
your mind disturbed, Mathieu, my son, do you need me
to straighten it out? In any case what is all this talk of
travelling? You don't speak any other languages – you
couldn't even be bothered to learn Latin.

Mathieu   I'll learn some languages.

Adrien   A true Frenchman doesn't learn foreign
languages. He is content with his own, which is quite
sufficient, complete, balanced and lovely to listen to; the
whole world envies us our language.

Mathieu   But I envy the whole of the rest of the world.

Adrien   Kindly wipe that suspicious look off your face,
Mathieu. (*He slaps* **Mathieu**'*s face.*) It's still there. (*He
gives him a second slap.*) At last I recognise my son again.

Mathieu   It makes no difference; I shall still be a
soldier.

Adrien   What did you say?

Mathieu   Is it true that I have flat feet?

Adrien   Of course it is, I told you. Look at mine. Is that
what is worrying you? But you can live with that,
Mathieu, my son. You just have to avoid wearing shoes

too often. But otherwise you are an ordinary man,
Mathieu, completely ordinary.

Mathieu I always wanted to be extraordinary.

Adrien That's foolish. There are more and more
people who are extraordinary. It has reached the point
where it has become something extraordinary to be
perfectly ordinary. So just be patient; you don't need to
do anything, nothing at all.

They leave.

II

Scene 5

Corridor; half-open door from which emerges **Adrien**,
followed, separately, by a few men, then by **Plantières**, *who
remains alone in the corridor.*
Enter **Edouard**, *who seizes hold of* **Plantières**.
Enter **Mathilde**, *holding scissors.*

Plantières Who are you? What do you want?

Mathilde I am Mathilde and I am about to shave off
your hair. I shall remove every last bristle from your
head. You will leave here with your skull as smooth as the
skull of a woman who has slept with the enemy. You will
taste the pleasure of going out into the streets with a head
that is lumpy and white. A naked skull is the worst kind of
nakedness. You are about to discover the unbearably slow
pace at which your hair grows back again. You will look
into the mirror in the morning and see only a disgusting
old man, a repulsive stranger, a monkey apeing your own
expressions. Then you will discover how hard it is to
cover a skull; you will hunt for hats and they will all seem
ghastly; you will dream of wigs and of toupées; you will

hate the people you see in the streets for looking so lovely, with their curls and their fine flowing locks; and for month after month your whole life, your thoughts, your dreams, your energy, your desires, your hatred, will all revolve around this ridiculous absence of hair on your head. You will concentrate to make it grow faster; you will tug on the first tufts to speed them up; and you will see that it doesn't speed them up at all, but that the rate of growth remains unbearably slow, and that the days are long, and the weeks are long and the months are long, and still you have to put up with this obscene skull, and you will long for it to have been your balls that were cut off.

Plantières   Who is this brat who is bullying me? I am an honourable man. I am a man who is respected and I have earned that respect. My career is blameless, my family life is impeccable, I am well respected in this town. I am not the sort of person who hangs around the streets at night and gets attacked by thugs. I only leave my home to go to visit friends, or to the police station, or to church. Am I no longer safer in a friend's house? Should I be anxious about straying from home? Must I expect, soon, to be afraid of violence in my own house? Why are you so worked up about my hair? What has it done to you? I shall soon be old and then it will fall out all by itself. I want it to fall out by itself, I won't have it touched.

Mathilde   It was the same with me, I didn't want mine touched. But you picked me out in front of the crowd, you pointed your finger at me, you got them to spit at me with your slanders, you accused me of treason. Yes, you. And even if you have forgotten, even if time has passed, I have not forgotten.

Plantières   But what are you talking about and who on earth do you think I am? Something happened to you in the distant past, long ago, and you've mistaken me for someone else. As for me, I don't know you, I've never set eyes on you, and you don't know me either. You must have broken in through the window with this brat who is tearing my arm from my shoulder. Are you burglars? If so, you should know that it's not my house, I can't help you; I'll even promise not to get in your way, not to raise the alarm. Are you a servant? If so, you should be aware that you are as good as fired. No, I rather think you must be just some crazy old bat they keep locked in the attic, a family legacy. How did you escape? Help! Help! Make this animal let go of me!

Mathilde   I am no longer old and I have never been a servant. I am Mathilde and this is my house. It is mine, and there is every reason for you not to feel safe in it. I know you. I recognise you. Fifteen years have fattened you up; they have clothed you in luxury and placed spectacles on your nose; they have encrusted your fingers with rings. But even if a hundred years had passed between the day when you pointed me out and condemned me to exile, and today when you will be punished for it, even if three hundred years had passed, I should still recognise you.

Plantières   You don't even know my name.

Mathilde   What do I care about your name? It's your hair I'm after.

Plantières   Well let me tell you this, and you had better believe me. I come from a large family; I have at least seven brothers and we all look alike; I have hundreds of cousins, who could all be mistaken for me; in my family we intermarry a lot and so every new baby looks like all the others, in fact the mothers often don't know which one is which. It's someone else you're looking for, someone else. Examine me carefully, the light isn't good here. Do you really recognise this cheek? And what about the little scar under my ear, have you ever seen that before? Are you certain you recognise the shape of my nose? Look at me carefully. You're mistaken, you're mistaken. I'm not the one you're after.

Mathilde *cuts off all his hair.*

Mathilde You're the one, we recognise you.

Mathilde *and* **Edouard** *leave.*

Plantières Adrien, help! (*Enter* **Adrien**.) Mr
Serpenoise, you got here too late. Mr Serpenoise, we're
no longer on first-name terms, our friendship is finished.
There will be no more invitations to the Prefecture and no
more favours. How dare you smile? Yes, yes, I saw a
smile, a dirty sneer on your face. Don't look at me. Have
the decency to turn away, look down at your feet, Mr
Serpenoise, those feet of yours, which go wandering
naked into every polite household in this town: they're
just as ridiculous as my head. What is the point of this
behaviour? You could at least wear socks or slippers. And
you think you have the right to smile! I thought that this
was the home of a friend, a colleague. I thought we
understood one another You have deceived me, but what
a long time it took for you to come out in your true
colours! Your family are all mad. A hysterical sister, a boy
who is weak in the head, practically a mongol, a nephew
and a niece who are sick, depressive, epileptic. How could
I have thought, how could all the decent people in this
town have thought that you could escape from the
degenerate influences of your family? And now you're
sneering; you are showing yourself for what you really
are; you have betrayed me, Mr Serpenoise. And to think
that we chose your house, the house of a madman and a
traitor, to hold these meetings which expose us all to such
dangers. I shall make sure the others are warned; every
door will be closed to you and you will be cut dead. You
will be banned from the OAS. We were stupid to trust
you, and you may even be punished. You will pay for this,
Serpenoise; you are a traitor.

Adrien Calm down Plantières. I did not smile. It was
an expression of shame: my family's a heavy burden. But
what can I do about it? I am not responsible for my sister;
I cannot just kill her. With your help, Plantières, I did
everything I could to keep her away from here. But I

cannot be expected to kill her. I will compensate you for this terrible accident.

Plantières What about my wife? And my children? And my colleagues at the Prefecture?

Adrien Take a holiday for a few weeks, take my country cottage. Mathilde, Mathilde, I almost feel I *could* kill her, and her children with her. I could commit murder, yes, but I give you my oath, Archibald, that I am not a traitor.

Plantières Yes you are, you have betrayed me, Adrien.

Adrien I swear to you that I am not; I have never said a word.

Plantières How did she know, then? You are the one who begged me to accuse her of fraternising with the enemy; I gave in, out of sheer folly, and that became our secret. You told her, Serpenoise, there is no other explanation.

Adrien I did not tell her, I swear it on the head of my son, whom I love. No one knew apart from you and me. And Marie.

Plantières Marie is dead.

Adrien Yes, Marie is dead. Plantières, you must take revenge, and I know how. You are the chief of police; call together Borny, the lawyer, and Sablon, the prefect of the département. Mathilde's daughter is a lunatic; she is convinced she has seen ghosts in the garden at night. It gives us the perfect excuse to section her. Let's hide in the garden one evening; we can be witnesses to her madness and we shall both be revenged, my poor Archibald.

They leave.

Scene 6: Zohr

In the drawing room.
Enter **Maame Queuleu** *and* **Mathilde.**

Maame Queuleu Now come along Mathilde. You must make it up with your brother; your arguments have turned this house into a living hell. And for what, dear God, for what? Just because something has been put in a place you don't want it put, or because Master Adrien don't like your style of dressing and you don't like this habit of going around barefoot. Are you still children? Can't you find a compromise? Don't you know that growing up means just that, finding compromises, giving up obstinacy and being content with what you can get? Grow up, Mathilde, grow up, it is high time. All this squabbling just gives you wrinkles, horrid, ugly wrinkles. Do you want to be covered with ugly wrinkles because of some fuss that you can't even remember a few minutes after? I will help you to find a compromise, Mathilde, I'm good at that: the master gets up at six and you at ten; well, you both get up at eight. You hate pork and he only likes roasts; well, I'll cook you both roast veal. Life could be easy if you only wanted. Make it up with him, Mathilde, this house is becoming impossible.

Mathilde I have no intention of making it up, since I was never cross with him.

Maame Queuleu Shut up; I can hear your brother's outbursts from here. What have you done to him? Why do the mornings always have to start with shouting and the evenings end in sulks? Is this the rhythm of your blood? Well it's not mine, it's not mine at all and I'll never get used to it. Just one angry outburst like yours and I would be sick, exhausted. But anger just seems to make you stronger. Your energy wears me out much more than housework. Put your energy into something else, my girl, do some sewing or embroidery or carpentry. And let the master get back to looking after his factory; they say in town that it's all gone to rack and ruin since your return. Do you want to be ruined? Answer me, Mathilde, your silence frightens me.

Mathilde Embroidery, Maame Queuleu? Can you see me doing embroidery? Quiet, I can hear him coming.

Maame Queuleu Have some pity on us, Mathilde, have some pity.

Enter **Marthe**.

Marthe I have calmed him down, thank God. I know a special prayer, guaranteed to make the demon tremble with awe; I flung it in his face and he vanished at once. Now my little Adrien is sweet-tempered again, but tired, for the demon tires him out.

Mathilde This woman has been at the bottle already, at this time of day. Why can't she drink tea, like everyone else? We ought to have her put in a clinic.

Marthe My little Mathilde, you must be kind to my poor Adrien; he's a child, he's clumsy, but he loves you so much, and of course you deserve it.

Mathilde Maame Queuleu, can you not get rid of this woman?

Marthe (*to* **Maame Queuleu**) Bring us something to drink; our two angels are reconciled to one another and we must celebrate it.

Maame Queuleu I can't hear your brother any more. It sounds as though he really has calmed down.

Enter **Adrien**.

Maame Queuleu Adrien, your sister is ready to kiss and make up.

Adrien I will kiss her later.

Maame Queuleu Why not now?

Adrien First I have a couple of things to say. She has set all my friends against me. She insults them, mistreats them, so that they no longer dare to visit me, and when I meet them in the street they greet me with reproaches. Why should they reproach me for the follies of this woman? I refuse to pay for her any more.

Mathilde   Everything about them sets my teeth on edge, Maame Queuleu, I can't help it. Besides, Adrien infuriates me as well. The noise of his feet in the corridor, his habit of coughing, his way of saying 'my son', those little secret meetings with no women allowed. Why should I have to keep out of a room in my own house for hours on end? Why should they come here to lay their plots? I am going to have all the doors in this house removed so that I can see whatever is going on, whenever I choose; I want to be able to come and go freely at any hour of the day or night.

Maame Queuleu   Mathilde, you promised.

Mathilde   All in good time, Maame Queuleu.

Adrien   They are saying in town that she walks around naked on her balcony.

Maame Queuleu   Don't be silly; Mathilde, naked, on her balcony!

Adrien   That's what they say.

Maame Queuleu   They say whatever comes into their heads.

Adrien   If they say that she goes around naked on her balcony it's as good as if I had seen it myself. Nobody says that sort of thing about me or about you, Maame Queuleu. Even as a young girl she behaved like a fallen woman, it's in her nature; no chance of her being miraculously changed into a lady at this late stage.

Marthe   There is always the chance of a miracle, we must believe that.

Mathilde   Fallen woman, Maame Queuleu? And what about his son? Can you imagine a more outrageous example of original sin? Why did he have to do it? What right has he got to clutter up my house with his useless and lazy progeny? He just lounges around all day long in the garden or the drawing room. It was bad enough having Adrien on our backs, the last thing I needed was

his double bumbling around the corridors, a second
Adrien, a caricature of the first. Why, ask him why he had
to go and get married, Maame Queuleu, and why he had
to father that child.

Adrien   Ask her, Maame Queuleu, why she had two.

Mathilde   You just tell him that I wasn't responsible for
making them.

Adrien   Her son hangs about in the Arab cafés, out in
the slums; everyone knows that. It's in his blood. The
Algerian sun has turned my sister's head and lo and
behold she has gone native and her son with her. I will not
have my son being dragged off to the slums, I will not
have him going into Arab cafés.

Marthe   They do say in town that the Arabs give
poisoned sweets to young boys and girls and that they end
up in Marrakesh, in the houses of ill repute.

Adrien   Besides, she will end up denouncing my son to
the military authorities. He has been seen wandering
around in town. She is more than capable of doing it
because she wants the factory and so she thinks she can
send my son off to be massacred in Algeria. But she'll
never have the factory, never, never!

Maame Queuleu   Stop it, both of you! Mathilde, you
are the oldest. Kiss your brother; do that for me.

Mathilde   I will kiss him directly, Maame Queuleu. But
did you know he had hit me? This very morning, while I
was drinking my tea, he struck at me and the teapot was
smashed into bits. Should I put up with that?

Marthe   It was when the demon was in him.

Maame Queuleu (*to* **Adrien**)   Is it true that you struck
her? Why did you do that?

Adrien   I no longer know, but I must have had a reason
and a good one too. I do not strike out wildly.

Maame Queuleu   Is that all? Well then, make it up.
Adrien, you promised me.

Adrien   Right away, soon, presently. But just one more thing: did you know, Maame Queuleu, that yesterday she hit my wife? My poor Marthe, she hit her.

Marthe   No, no, she did not hit me.

Adrien   I saw her, I heard the slap and she still had the mark after several hours.

Marthe   She did not hit me, she chastised me for my wickedness. It was for my own good and I am contented.

Mathilde   Imbecile.

Adrien (*to* **Mathilde**)   What did you say? (*He moves towards* **Mathilde**.)

Maame Queuleu   All right then, go ahead, hit, mutilate, put out one another's eyes, just get it over with. I'll go and get you a knife to speed things up. Aziz, get me the big kitchen knife, in fact get two while you're at it; I sharpened them myself this morning, they'll do the job quick. Scratch, claw and kill, once and for all, but at least shut up, or else I shall personally cut out your tongues, slice them off at the roots, right at the back of your throats, so I don't have to hear your voices. Then you can fight on in silence; at least no one will know and we shall be able to live again. For you only fight with words, words, useless words, which hurt everyone except yourselves. If only I could be deaf, all that would not upset me. It doesn't bother me if you want to fight, but do it in silence so that the wounds are not felt by all of us, who live around you, in our bodies and in our heads. Each day your voices become louder and shriller, they pierce the walls, they turn the milk sour in the kitchen. We long for the evening, when you're sulking; at least then we can work. I pray for the sun to set earlier every day and for them to hate one another in silence. I give up.

Mathilde (*to* **Adrien**)   I said: imbecile. She is dead drunk. In a minute she will be sick all over the carpet.

Adrien *hits her.*

Maame Queuleu   Aziz, Aziz! (**Mathilde** *hits* **Adrien**.) Edouard, Aziz, help! (*Enter* **Aziz**.) Aziz, separate them. Come on, move. What are you waiting for, Aziz? Move.

Aziz   No, I will not move, I am not paid to move. If I did, they would blame me; and if I do nothing, they will still blame me, so I prefer to do nothing – like that I shall take the blame but not the strain.

Maame Queuleu   Aziz, look at them.

Aziz   I can see them, Maame Queuleu, I can see them. But what does it matter if the old fools want to quarrel, and why should I care? They don't even see me; they are so blinded by their anger that their eyes are closed to me. And when their anger has left them, I will be the last thing they notice, after all the broken vases. So let them beat each other up, and when they have calmed down, Aziz will pick up the pieces.

Enter **Edouard**.

Maame Queuleu   Edouard, I beg you, I'm going mad.

Edouard *restrains his mother,* **Aziz** *restrains* **Adrien**.

Adrien   You are mad, do you think you can defy the whole world? Who are you to go around provoking respectable people? Who are you to make fun of polite society, criticise other people's behaviour, accuse and slander and swear at everyone you meet? You are nothing but a woman, a woman with no fortune, an unmarried mother, a child-mother; not long ago, you would have been banned from polite society. We should have spat in your face and shut you up in a secret place as if you had never existed. What rights can you claim? Our father forced you to eat your meals kneeling down for a year because of your sin, but the punishment was much too mild. We should still force you to go down on your knees when you eat at our table, you should go down on your knees when you talk to me, down on your knees in front of my wife, in front of Maame Queuleu, in front of your children, Who do you think you are, and what do you take us for, that you continue to curse us like this; do you think you can declare war on everyone?

Mathilde   Yes, Adrien, I am declaring war, on you, on your son, and on your apology for a wife. I defy everyone in this house, and the garden that surrounds it and the tree where my daughter was damned and the wall running round the garden. I defy the lot of you, the air you breathe, the rain that falls on your heads and the ground you walk on. I defy this town, every one of its streets and every single house. I defy the river running through it, the canal and its barges; I defy the sky that is above your heads, the birds in the sky, the dead buried beneath you, the dead already mingling with the earth and the unborn babies in their mothers' wombs. And I do so because I know that I am stronger than all of you, Adrien.

Aziz *drags* **Adrien** *away,* **Edouard** *drags* **Mathilde** *away. But they break free and come back.*

Mathilde   And another thing, the reason why the factory isn't mine is because I didn't want it, because a factory can go broke in no time, but a house decays slowly, and this house will still be standing long after my death and my children's deaths, when all your boy will have left to do is wander through your deserted stockrooms, while the rain pours through the roof, repeating: it's mine, it's mine. No, the factory may be yours, but this house belongs to me, and because it belongs to me, I have decided that you will leave tomorrow. You will take your bags, your son and all your other clutter, especially your clutter, and you will go off and live in your warehouses, in your offices with their crumbling plaster and piles of rotting stock. Tomorrow I take possession of my own home.

Adrien   What do you mean by rotting stock and crumbling plaster and decay? My turnover has never been higher. Do you think I need this house? Certainly not. I only liked living here because of our father; it was in his memory and out of love for him.

Mathilde Our father? Out of love for our father? I chucked that out with the rubbish a long time ago.

Adrien No Mathilde, not that, have a little respect, you could at least avoid smearing filth on that.

Mathilde No, I won't smear filth on it: it's filthy enough as it is.

Adrien I will kill her.

Edouard (*dragging* **Mathilde** *away*) Stop it Maman, come with me.

Aziz (*dragging* **Adrien** *away*) Madame, the master is very angry. She doesn't know what she's saying. No one would talk like that about their father if they knew what they were saying.

They leave, but then **Mathilde** *and* **Adrien** *break free and come back.*

Adrien (*being restrained by* **Aziz**) You will pay for that one, you will pay for it.

Mathilde Do you think I couldn't pay if I wanted to? But you won't get a thing.

Aziz Sir, my arms are hurting from holding you back. Do you want to force me to knock you out? (*He drags* **Adrien** *off.*)

Adrien I will kill her.

Adrien *and* **Aziz** *leave.*

Edouard Maman, if I have to, I'll force you out.

Mathilde Tomorrow, he goes.

Edouard *and* **Mathilde** *leave.*

Maame Queuleu Marthe, my poor child, how unhappy we are. They were so loving when they were little.

Marthe Bring me something to drink, I am so tired. Josephine, I beg you, go and get me a bottle of port.

Maame Queuleu It's too early, my little one.

Marthe Ah, Josephine, Josephine, my dear friend. If you weren't there, the world would collapse. Deliver me from this hell, I beg you. You are a saint. When we are both dead, when you are in heaven and I'm in hell because of all the evil things I've done, throw me a rope and draw me up to you; for if you don't do it, who will? My sister Marie won't even look at me, all the others have too many troubles of their own to remember me and Aziz, generous Aziz, will be in limbo, because he hasn't been baptised, and there's no communication between hell and limbo. Don't leave me to be forgotten in hell after I've been forgotten here all my short life. Promise me that you'll draw me up, Josephine.

Maame Queuleu I don't know, my poor Marthe; I don't know if there is a heaven.

Marthe What did you say?

Maame Queuleu If there was a heaven, we'd at least get an echo of it, a tiny impression, a hint of heaven on earth, some little scraps or reflections. But there's nothing, except scraps of hell.

Marthe Come on, let's get a drink.

They leave.

Scene 7

Far away the sound of soldiers from the parachute regiment singing a bawdy song as they march.

Adrien (*to the audience*) Mathilde says I'm not quite a man, I'm an ape. Perhaps I'm just the same as everyone else: halfway between ape and man. Possibly I'm a little more ape than she is and perhaps Mathilde is a little more human than me. She is certainly cleverer, but I hit harder. I am quite content with my condition as an old ape squatting at the feet of a human and keeping watch. I have never wanted to play at being human, and don't intend to start now. Besides, I wouldn't know how – you see, I've met so few.

When my son was born, I had a high wall built all round the house. I didn't want this ape-child to see the forest with its insects and wild animals, its traps and its hunters. The only time I put on my shoes is when I have to go with him on an outing, to protect him in the jungle. The happiest apes are the ones born and bred in a cage, with a good keeper, who die believing that the whole world is like their cage. That's the best way. That's ape-salvation. At least I shall have protected my own little baboon.

Secretly, apes love to observe humans, just as humans never stop glancing furtively at the apes. Because they belong to the same family, but at different stages, and neither knows which is ahead of the other. Nobody knows which is evolving towards which, no doubt because the ape moves constantly towards the condition of man, while man moves towards that of the ape, At all events, man has a greater need to observe the apes than to contemplate other men, and the apes need to contemplate men more than other apes. So there they are, keeping jealous watch, arguing, clawing, snapping at one another, but never breaking off, not even mentally, and never tiring of looking at one another.

When the Buddha visited the apes he sat down amongst them, in the evening, and said to them: 'Apes, behave yourselves well, behave like humans and not like apes, and one morning you will wake up as humans.' So the apes trusted him and behaved like humans: they made every effort to conduct themselves as they thought a human should. But the apes were too gentle and too stupid. Every evening they were full of hope and they went to sleep with sweet optimistic smiles. But every morning they woke up weeping.

I am an aggressive, brutal ape and I do not believe in the

Buddha's tales. I do not wish for evenings of hope as I
have no desire for tears in the morning.

III: 'Ichâ

Scene 8

In the garden; night.
Enter **Fatima** *and* **Mathieu.**

Fatima   Go away, Mathieu. Stop pressing yourself
against me. Ever since I first got here you've used any
excuse to rub up against me and touch me. Remember
we're cousins and it's wrong to touch me like you do when
we belong to the same family.

Mathieu   We do not belong to the same family. The
only reason for families is because of the inheritance, so
that it can pass from father to son. You will inherit
nothing from my father and I will inherit nothing from
you; so if I feel like touching you I don't see anything
wrong in that. We were not born from the same woman;
you don't even know your father but I know very well
who mine is. We have nothing in common. How far back
do you have to go to feel free? When do two people start
to be strangers? How many generations do you need
before the family ties are cut?

Fatima   The world is full of women. Why should I be
the one you have to squeeze and touch all the time? I
don't feel like it. Besides, cousin or no cousin, family or
not, I don't like being touched, not by anyone.

Mathieu   There aren't that many women.

Fatima   More than half the people in the world, and it's
me you choose to pester.

Mathieu   There ought to be two words for women,

then. Maame Queuleu is a woman. She goes up and down all day and I hardly even see her; even in my mind I can't see her any different from how she is, in ugly clothes with dusters in her hand. How can the same word, woman, be used for Maame Queuleu and for you, when there's no kind of resemblance between you? I look at you, even as you are, dressed up for mid-winter although the weather's so mild, and I see you differently, in my mind and in reality. What's more, I feel I want to look at you like I've never looked at any other woman.

Fatima   You're thirty and you've never looked at a woman?

Mathieu   I'm not quite thirty and I've seen lots of women in my life, starting with Maame Queuleu; I've seen her every day since I was born. But I've been short of women to look at for some time now because they've stopped coming to the house.

Fatima   Well go out, then, go out into the slums; there's lots of women there, women who you pay and then they let you look at them, and if you give them a bit more money, they even let you touch them. They'd be quite willing to do it, because you're not too bad looking and you've got plenty of money.

Mathieu   But I do go out, Fatima; I'm always going out. I've gone out a lot in my life. There's church for a start, and even the factory, which is a long way off, but which I have visited because I shall be the one to inherit it. But I haven't been out for a while now; I haven't got the time, and I haven't got that much money, either, not yet, anyway.

Fatima   Well I won't be the one who saves you time, or money. Go away, Mathieu. Here's Maman, and if she sees you with me, you can be sure you'll get a hammering.

Mathieu   Let her come if she wants! A good beating'll shut her up. She's been annoying me for long enough, the way she pries into everything. I'll show her who I am.

Enter **Mathilde**.

Mathilde   Fatima, I was looking for you. But I am relieved to see you are with your cousin. I like you to be friends, you two; Mathieu is a good boy, serious and thoughtful. This little tomboy could certainly do with some of that. Mathieu, my little Mathieu, it's a lovely evening, let's go out into the garden and walk together.

Mathieu   I should have liked to accept, Aunt Mathilde, for I too enjoy your company. But I have to work, and I was just saying to Fatima that even though this mild weather is perfect for a stroll, if you're serious about your studies, you sometimes have to do without such pleasures.

Mathilde   Mathieu, Mathieu, if only you could transplant that idea into the brains of my two children. Go on then, I won't keep you away from your studies. (**Mathieu** *leaves*.) Fatima, I don't like you hanging about in this garden at night. Fatima, I too hung about here a long time ago. I hung about one night too many and the result was your brother, and I didn't even see the face of the man who saddled me with that little gift. Fatima, there are people like that, who climb walls and who watch out for women who stray, and afterwards you land up with a gift you never wanted. The gardens of this town are dangerous, what with the barracks and its soldiers who climb the walls and distribute their gifts. Fatima, are you alone?

Fatima   I am alone, but I'm waiting for someone, and it's not a soldier from the barracks. You mustn't stay.

Mathilde   Let me see her, Fatima. I will hide over there and I won't make a noise, but let me see her. It's fifteen years since she died, and I haven't stopped missing her.

Fatima   Look, Maman, behind the walnut tree. Can you see a light?

Mathilde   I see nothing.

Fatima   Look hard. Can't you see a bit of her white dress? She's afraid to show herself.

Mathilde   Fatima, I can see nothing.

Fatima   Can't you feel a biting cold? A fearful cold?

Mathilde   Cold, yes, I can feel the cold; a fearful cold.

Fatima   It's her, it's Marie. Get further back: she's frightened.

Mathilde   Why should she be frightened? I am Mathilde, I am her best friend.

Fatima   She'll think I've betrayed her. Go away.

Mathilde   Marie, it's me, Mathilde. Surely you're not afraid of your old Mathilde? It's me, Marie, even though I have grown old. Forgive me for being so old. You died in time, but you always left me standing. (*To* **Fatima**.) Is she still there?

Fatima   She is there.

Mathilde   All of her? Can you see all of her?

Fatima   Yes, all of her now. She's all there and she's looking at you.

Mathilde   Are you quite sure?

Fatima   Yes, she's looking at you.

Mathilde   Let me alone, Marie. I don't want you looking at me or remembering me and I don't want to have to remember you. Why can't I get you out of my head, even when I beg you to leave? Why am I so helpless? I can just see you, with your chaste expression and your virgin innocence. That face has followed me everywhere, even when I was in the shit, especially when I was in the shit. What the hell were you doing there, always there, sticking close, always getting between Adrien and me, always sticking to Adrien? Well you had him; you grafted yourself onto him and you grafted yourself onto me; why do you have to hang onto us like this? How is it you could get inside my head, even in

Algeria, when you never left your house, except once to
cross the road and marry that ape you had been lusting
after for so long? And after that you never left his house
until you sneaked away, managed to duck out of life,
skedaddled so as not to soil your innocent little hands
with the shitty business of life. (*To* **Fatima**.) Is she still
there?

Fatima   She's there, and she's weeping.

Mathilde   Well then, let her weep, let her weep gallons!
That way the dead can at least serve some purpose, crying
with shame as they look at us. What's she got to complain
of? She's well set up. She knows where she lives, in the
country of virgins and saints. And since no one comes to
bother her, she spends her time annoying others. After
all, why should the dead suddenly turn into fine, virtuous,
respectable people, just by dying? I am sure she was never
as beautiful as all that, nor as nice as I remember her. In
any case, she wouldn't have stayed that way for long.

Fatima   She's going, Maman, she's turning away, she's
vanishing behind the tree.

Mathilde   Let her vanish, let her go and lie in her
cotton-wool bed, let her go and sing her hymns with the
angels and leave us here in our shit, alone, without house
or home or land.

Fatima   She's gone, Maman, you frightened her.

Fatima *leaves.*

Mathilde   What country do I belong to? Where is my
homeland, the ground on which I can rest in peace? In
Algeria I am a foreigner and I dream of France; in France
I am even more of a foreigner and I dream of Algiers.
Perhaps your home is the place you're not at? I'm fed up
with never being at home, never knowing where home is.
But there are no homelands, nowhere, no. Marie, if you
could die a second time, I would wish for your death.
Sing your hymns, wallow in your heaven, or your hell,
but stay wallowing, rid me of your presence.

Scene 9

Corridor. **Borny** *enters through a half-open door. After a moment, enter* **Plantières**.

Plantières   You're leaving, you're running away, Borny.

Borny   I'm not leaving, Plantières, I'm not leaving. I forgot to get something out of my car.

Plantières   What? What thing? What could you possibly need from your car?

Borny   My bag, my briefcase. I left my briefcase in the car.

Plantières   And so you were after your briefcase when you took advantage of the fact that no one was paying attention to slip away?

Borny   Slip away? What do you mean 'slip away'? It wasn't that at all. You see, normally I keep my glasses fixed to a cord round my neck and today I've mislaid the cord. I can't follow anything when I don't have my glasses and it was such an important discussion. Do you mind, Plantières, please let me just go and get my glasses.

Plantières   Ah, so now it's your glasses that you want to go and get? Have you any idea at all what it is you're looking for?

Borny   Yes, I am looking for my glasses, which are in my briefcase, which is in my car. This is an insult, Plantières.

Plantières   Far from it, Borny, but I must insist on accompanying you to your car.

Borny   And why should you accompany me?

Plantières   Just to make sure that you don't lose your way.

Borny   You doubt me, Plantières, and that wounds me.

Have I not said, several times, that your idea is excellent and has my full approval?

Plantières   Did you say 'your' idea? What do you mean by 'your'? I don't like the sound of that. Are you wriggling out of it by saying 'your'?

Borny   Not in the least bit. When the time comes I shall applaud wholeheartedly.

Plantières   Wholehearted applause, well now! Where will you be applauding? Will you be hidden away in your room, with the door firmly shut to prevent anyone hearing? Who will witness it? Your canary? What do we care for your applause?

Borny   Do you want a good hiding, Plantières?

Plantières   Go on, give me a good hiding.

Borny   I will, I swear it.

Plantières   Do it then, and stop swearing.

Enter (by the same door) **Adrien, Sablon,** *a few more men.*

Adrien   What's this noise, this row, this shambles?

Borny   Plantières is insulting me.

Plantières   Borny's trying to run off.

Borny   He's a liar.

Plantières   He's a coward.

Sablon   Please, gentlemen, please. I will not hear of rows in our organisation.

Plantières   Just at the moment when a decision has to be made, Monsieur le Préfet, Borny suddenly remembers that he's left his glasses in the car.

Adrien   His glasses? Do you wear glasses now, Borny?

Borny (*to* **Sablon**)   Monsieur le Préfet, please understand me. You know very well that I have never been one to hesitate when action calls. But this time, in my position, and it's in your own best interests too, I don't want to be involved, I mean not directly. You all know very well, gentlemen, that I am with you in spirit.

Plantières Where does the spirit come in? We don't need you to be with us in spirit. We need to blow up Saïfi's café.

Adrien Stop this shouting or I shall throw you all out.

Borny Very well then. Your intentions are excellent, no doubt. But take a good look at that hoodlum you've got to do the job. He'll blow up the café even if it's full of people. I don't want my conscience spattered with blood. Ah, my dear Adrien, think of the time when anarchists would rather go up with their own bomb than risk wounding a single child.

Sablon Quiet. Where do you think you are? Let's go back in the room.

Plantières You too, Borny.

Borny Plantières, I swear I shall give you a hiding.

Plantières Go on then, swear, it hurts a lot less than a hiding.

Sablon Borny, shut up.

Borny Why me? Why always me?

Adrien Silence!

They go into the room. **Adrien** *closes the door.*

Scene 10

The boundary wall. Night time. **Mathieu** *and* **Edouard**.

Mathieu What a wonderful world and how beautiful it all is. Even this wall seems to have been made expressly so that I should enjoy the pleasure of climbing out. Look, Edouard: night is falling and this fine fat town is settling down to sleep like a tired old woman; it's all ours. And now you tell me there are even places where you can see women who let you touch them? Here, in this town? For more than twenty-five years I've lived here, and never knew that, and you've discovered it right away. Good old Edouard, your muscles may not be developed, but your head is. So don't tell me the world is a mess. Feel the warmth, feel how it arouses all your senses. Just think what a bore if it was the cold that got you worked up, and the winter, so that you had to satisfy your senses while you were all bogged down in heavy clothing and fits of the shivers. No, the world is well made: warm air appeals to the warmth of the beast and because of the warmth in the air the beast gets rid of its clothes and then, Edouard, the naked beast is ready for business. Let's go, Edouard.

Edouard Even the smallest village has its brothel, you arsehole, and the ones round here won't disappear if we take our time. Anyway, we must wait for Aziz to take us down to Cairo Road – that's where the best ones are. All I did was ask Aziz, like you could have done any time in the last twenty-five years. But it's true that for all your big muscles your brain is minute; I can't think how you've managed for so long. Even so, you don't look that bad, you seem healthy enough.

Mathieu You're right, young Edouard, healthy is what I am. Look at how I hopped up onto the wall. I could do that ten times over in the time it would take you to climb it. Strength is important: what's the use of a swollen head, what's the use of being a clever-dick if you break up easily? Come here, young Edouard, I will lift you over and put you down on the other side and you won't feel a thing; and nor will I: you're as light as a baby. Look at these muscles, look how I keep them in trim. The women will love them. Poor Edouard, why don't you pay a bit more attention to your body? How can you hope to tempt the women with your rickety little arms and your scrawny neck? Since you are now my friend, Edouard, I shall take your training in hand. Given a few months and a bit of patience, we should be able to double the size of your shrimpy little body.

Edouard I'm not going to double anything. I'm OK as I am. I make out well enough with my body just as it is. In any case that body you take so much care of is constantly being replaced; those cells you keep in trim with such enormous effort will be washed away with soap and water tomorrow. After seven years, not one bit will be left of the body you have today; you will have wasted your time spending two hours a day in training.

Mathieu Seven years is a long time, and my two hours of training will at least have helped me to please the women. I'm going to please them and that's for sure. Come on, let's move, Edouard.

Edouard Aziz isn't here yet.

Mathieu I'm fed up with Aziz; he's a gloomy old moaner. Even when he's off to have fun he looks so depressed that, if he hadn't told me otherwise, I would think he hates women. Why does he have to make going to the brothel look like a chore?

Edouard When you've done it a few times, you too will find that each time you go with a bit less speed and a bit less excitement.

Mathieu Well if we've got to wait, let's do something, let's work out, let's lift some rocks, let's do some hard labour. I get a kick from that kind of pain and suffering. Come on, work! work!

Enter **Aziz**.

Aziz If you go on behaving like apes on top of that wall you'll wake the whole district. Shut up, I don't want any trouble from your families.

Mathieu Aziz, my dear Aziz, if you like women why do you look so gloomy?

Aziz I never said I like women, I said I fucked them.

Mathieu   Well we're going anyway, Aziz, and the world is beautiful.

Aziz   I don't know about the world, but I know that you'll wake up your families. Come on. I can see lights being put on in one of the bedrooms.

Mathieu   That's Maame Queuleu's room. The old woman suffers from insomnia: she's sorry for her lost youth and her failure to enjoy it.

Aziz   I'll take you down to Cairo Road and then I'll leave you: I'm not going with a woman today. I'll wait for you at Saïfi's café: it's just round the corner.

Edouard   Come with us, Aziz, I don't want to be left alone with this idiot.

Aziz   Hurry, hurry. Another light has just come on. I'm not part of the family and I'll get the sack if they find me leading you astray.

Mathieu   It's your mother, Edouard; I think she's going to see if you're still tucked up in bed with your teddy bear. Run, Edouard, Mummy's coming to the window.

Edouard   And what about that other window where the light's just come on, whose room is that?

Mathieu   That's Papa's room. Let's go.

They leave.

Scene 11

Veranda. **Adrien.**
The **Great Black Parachutist** *appears.*

Parachutist   Everyone in the house is asleep, Colonel.

Adrien   Don't call me Colonel; I'm not in the armed forces. Who are you? How did you get in?

Parachutist   This town seems very sleepy to me, bourgeois. Is it deserted?

Adrien How did you get in?

Parachutist I dropped in from the sky, of course. We came tonight; the army is here, bourgeois. Not the army crawling along on the cobbles, not the one that drives around protected by armour, nor the one that chatters in offices, not the army of latrine-diggers, but the one that keeps watch between the earth and the sky. As for me, I floated down like a little snowflake in summer time, so that you could sleep safe and sound. For you don't rely on the thickness of your walls to keep you safe, do you? You don't think that your wealth can protect you? All that could be shattered in pieces by a single shot placed right between your eyes.

Adrien You've been drinking, soldier. I shall have a word with your officers.

Parachutist You can have your words, bourgeois, but I must be respected.

Adrien I respect you my lad, but why so aggressive? Didn't you say you had come to keep me safe?

Parachutist First there must be turmoil if you want to obtain safety.

Adrien Well then, welcome, welcome, soldier! I keep an orderly household and I respect the army.

Parachutist So you should: the army makes you rich.

Adrien And don't forget I pay for you, soldier.

Parachutist Less than you pay for your servant, less than nothing. Just enough to buy cigarettes. But I'm the one who allows you to get fat and to scheme and to play at politics. We soldiers are the heart and lungs of the world and you, bourgeois, you are its intestines.

Adrien You are very wound up, my lad.

Parachutist Wound up, aroused, excited, yes.

Adrien Well then, I welcome your excitement! But you must know that this little town is a sleepy, quiet town, on good terms with its soldiers. The place for you soldiers is behind the barrack walls. Be good, keep quiet and the town will love you, the town will care for you. Now go back to your barracks.

Parachutist   Where are the women?

Adrien   I beg your pardon.

Parachutist   The women? Females, chicks, birds, broads, beavers, pussies, where have you hidden them? I can smell them; I can tell by the smell that there's tail somewhere round here. Out of my way, bourgeois.

Adrien   Calm down, my lad, calm down.

Parachutist   We won't be calm. We're here, bourgeois. Where are the women?

Adrien   There are only ladies here.

Parachutist   Don't worry, old man, I'll make women of them. Hide your mares, the army has loosed its stallions.

Adrien   Don't you love this country? Don't you love this land? What are you? A savage come to plunder or a soldier to protect it?

Parachutist   I love this land, bourgeois, but I don't love the people in it. Who is the enemy? Are you friend or foe? Who should I defend? Who should I attack? Since I don't know who is the enemy, I shoot everything that moves.

I love this land, sure, but I long for the good old days. I'm nostalgic for the soft light of oil lamps, for the glory of a navy under sail. I look back to the colonial era with its cool verandas and its croak of bull-frogs, when evenings were long and when everyone in the country knew his place, stretched out in a hammock, swinging on the rocking-chair or crouching beneath the mangrove, each in his own place, calm and settled, and that place was his. I'm nostalgic for the little nigger boys running about behind their cows, which you could send flying

like mosquitoes. Yes, I love this land, let no one doubt
it, I love my France all the way from Dunkirk to
Brazzaville because I have mounted guard on its
borders, I have marched for night after night, gun in
hand, ears cocked and eyes towards the foe. And now
I'm told I must forget nostalgia, that the times have
changed. I'm told that the borders move like the crest of
the waves; but whoever died for the march of the waves?
I'm told a nation can exist one moment and not the next,
that a man can find his place and then lose it again, that
the names of towns and estates and houses, and of the
people in the houses, can change in the course of a
lifetime, and then everything is reshuffled in a different
order, and then no one knows his name, nor his house,
nor his country, nor its borders. He no longer knows
what it is that he's meant to guard. He no longer knows
who is the enemy. He no longer knows who gives the
orders. I'm told that men must obey history, but a man's
life is infinitely too short, and history is like a great
sleepy cow: when she's done with chewing the cud, she
stamps her foot impatiently. My only function is to
fight, and my only rest is in death.

He disappears.

Adrien How on earth did he get in?

IV: Maghrib

Scene 12: By the bedside

Mathilde's *bedroom.*
Mathilde *and* **Fatima** *in bed.*

Mathilde Fatima, Fatima, are you asleep? I can hear
your uncle's footsteps in the corridor. He's coming
nearer, he's outside the door, he's hesitating. He means to

harm me. With no witnesses, at night, he'll dare to do what he hadn't the courage for in daylight. Move, Fatima, grunt, stir, talk to me, show him you're here. And if he comes in, open your eyes up wide and don't stop looking at him, let him understand you're awake. And if he's blinded by anger, so he can't see you, get up and wave. Everyone thinks you're mad, so it won't bother anyone. Fatima, my darling, stop sleeping, or pretending to; your uncle's outside the door and I'm scared.

You think I'm off my trolley, but it's not true, Fatima, I promise you. This town is full of people who die smothered by pillows, strangled by curtain cords, then there are the sadists who climb in through your windows and burglars who come for your pearls. And your uncle knows quite enough doctors and police officers to be protected from any risk. No one would know a thing. Goodbye Mathilde – just like Marie – snuffed out. How could anyone know how people die in this town? Right now the whole town is snoring with its eyes well closed, except for the murderers and their victims.

You're not asleep; I know how a person breathes when they're asleep. Have you ever had to go through a room with people asleep in it at night? Fatima, if you want to be disgusted by men, slip into their rooms, watch them and listen while they sleep. Why do they bother to dress up so respectably in the daytime, when half of their life is spent wallowing like pigs in a pond, unconscious, with no control over themselves, emptier than a tree trunk drifting on the river, with their eyeballs revolving in their sockets, or so I'm told. And then, once they're awake, they've forgotten all about it. This is a terrifying time of night, when the whole of humanity sweats into its sheets and thousands of people are there, all belching and spitting and grinding their teeth and sighing with closed eyes, digesting and digesting, clearing their throats, with their mouths wide open, pointing up at the ceiling. They're quite right to shut themselves away when they sleep. Every man should carry around with him, every day, the shame of the night he's just spent, the shame of abandoning himself to sleep. As for me, I never shut my door because I never sleep. I should have shut it; I can hear your uncle tramping about outside.

Fatima, if he comes in – I think he's going to come in – sit up suddenly and ask him how she died. The surprise might just jolt him into telling the truth before his lips are sealed once more by his own wickedness. I'm scared, my darling, my little daughter. Before he comes in – he's going to come in – hide yourself under the bed, and when he starts to stifle me with the pillow, pull hard on his feet so that he falls over. Fatima, my darling, don't leave me alone; show me a streak of light beneath your eyelids so that I can be sure you're not asleep. I'm really scared now. I'm so scared.

Enter **Adrien**.

Adrien   Mathilde, are you asleep? So much the better. Mathieu is off to do his military service. They finally caught up with him. I think my friends must have deserted me completely. Unless you're behind it. That's likely; no smoke without a fire. In any case, he's leaving for Algeria. He'll be massacred in some hole and they'll bring back the bits with military honours. Then I shall have no heir. But I warn you, old girl, you will never get the factory.

At first I almost went off to the graveyard to shoot myself in the head, like our grandfather did when his son went off into the army, and like our great-grandfather did for our grandfather. It's a family tradition, and traditions must be respected. But I decided against it, first of all because my father didn't do it for me, and then because it's raining and my shoes pinch, but mostly because the factory would have passed to you and that is something I will not have.

I don't like your children. You have trained them badly. Children need to be trained with kicks and wise precepts, or else they shit on your shoes at the first opportunity.

They shit on your shoes, old girl, and don't count on me to clean it up.

Mathieu is dead, or at all events he's as good as: he might as well be lying murdered in an Algerian ditch for all I care. I refuse to take an interest in a future corpse and I'm not the kind to weep over his tomb with 'if onlys'. The imminent corpse of my son is of no interest to me. So I shall become my own heir; I declare myself to be sole legatee and no one else will touch a penny of my inheritance.

Traditions must be respected. In our family the women die young, and frequently for no apparent cause. It's high time you followed suit. As Maame Queuleu says, you're still young. To say someone's still young really means they're growing old. Perhaps you'll choose to hang yourself from a tree in the garden, like Aunt Armelle; or throw yourself in the canal, quite without warning, after folding your clothes carefully on the bank, like the sweetly discreet and taciturn Ennie. Otherwise you'll end up smothered under a pillow in the normal way for women who are a nuisance. Such events never make the headlines: the authorities here are indulgent. It's one of the town's oldest traditions: we all have understanding friends. At least I think so. I'm afraid my friends may be deserting me. It's your fault: you've brought nothing but chaos since your return. It's impossible to live like this in a town without friends.

You hit out too much, Mathilde. One day you'll have a disaster, old girl. You're already cracked like an old jug: one day you'll shatter into pieces. You hit too hard, Mathilde, you shouldn't upset a quiet little town, nor should you provoke a peaceful family. You have travelled too much, old girl; travels disturb the mind, they distort your outlook. You think you are the stronger and already you are full of cracks. If the stone falls on the jug, too bad for the jug; if the jug falls on the stone, too bad for the jug.

And you are the jug, Mathilde. Are you in such a hurry to discover eternal life?

I don't like you despising my wife. I understand you annoying me and coveting my inheritance, that's in our blood, it's part of the tradition. But I will not have you despising my wife. She's as good as the other, yes, just as good as the other. Besides, I hesitated for a long time which one to choose; then I married the elder out of respect for the proprieties. In the end, I also married the younger; that way, there's nothing left to marry. But I forbid you to despise her, Mathilde; do that, and I could very well kill you.

I like you best when you're asleep: you keep your mouth shut and don't start getting at me. You listen quietly to what I tell you, as a sister ought to listen when her brother speaks. Maybe I had better sleep in the daytime and live at night; that way we should be the perfect brother and sister. Meanwhile, sleep on, Mathilde, your sleep protects you.

Exit.

Fatima   Christ, Maman, if Edouard behaved like that with me, I promise you I'd belt him one, I'd lay him out cold, he wouldn't try that again. Why do you let the men get away with it? They're full of shit, they're bluffing, they're empty windbags. Women are the strap that holds up the men's pants; if they let go, the men are bollock-naked. Your brother would be bollock-naked if you let go. Why won't you let go? What do you get out of it, apart from the excuse to ignore your children? You don't even see us any more, you're too busy rowing, and Edouard, poor Edouard is losing his mind, he's got a screw loose, he's all over the place, and you don't seem to notice a thing. Don't you give a damn?

Maman, I want to go back to Algeria. I don't understand the people here. I hate this house, I hate the garden and the street, all the houses and all the streets. It's cold at night, it's cold in the day. The cold frightens me more than the war. Why do you want to stay here when you just row with your brother all day? In Algeria you didn't row with anyone, I liked you better in Algeria than in France: you were stronger and we loved each other. Did you come back because you love rowing? Tell me: is it that you love rowing? Is that it? Why do we have to stay here and freeze, when we were so happy there? I was born there and I want to go back; I don't want to suffer in a foreign land, Maman. Maman, are you asleep? For good?

Scene 13: I won't go

In the kitchens.

Mathieu   Aziz, help me.

Aziz   That's what I'm doing; I'm working for your father and for you.

Mathieu   Not that kind of help, Aziz. Help me, old man.

Aziz   How else can I help you?

Mathieu   They want to send me off to the war. I've had my call-up papers; I'm supposed to be doing my military service.

Aziz   Everybody has to do military service. You're born, you suck, you grow, you smoke in secret, you get beaten by your father, you do your military service, you work, you marry, you have children, you grow old and you die full of wisdom. That's how everybody's life is.

Mathieu   But they'll send me to Algeria, Aziz. I don't want to fight. I don't want to die. How can I marry and have children and grow old and wise if I'm going to die?

Aziz   That's the price you pay for all the privileges you enjoy. For me it was different: I didn't have a father so I did my military service at the normal time. The war hadn't started, so I did it quietly at Commercy.

Mathieu   What's the army like, Aziz?

Aziz It's not that bad. Early to bed and early to rise, lots of sport, plenty of mates, leave to look forward to, no money worries, you don't have to think for yourself. It's good, very good.

Mathieu I shouldn't have to do military service: I've got flat feet. Why should I have to do it when the rule is that people with flat feet get off?

Aziz Flat feet? You?

Mathieu My father has them, so I have them too. It's inescapable.

Aziz If they've said you must do your military service it either means that you haven't got flat feet, or it means that people with flat feet do it just like everyone else. It's either one or the other. It's inescapable.

Mathieu How long does a war go on for?

Aziz Ages, I think.

Mathieu How long?

Aziz Once it gets going, no one knows when it'll stop. Perhaps it'll still be going for your children.

Mathieu If I die in the war I won't have any children.

Aziz Perhaps you won't die. Not everyone dies in a war.

Mathieu And what about wounds, Aziz? What if I come back an invalid?

Aziz Not everyone's wounded in a war. Perhaps you'll come back all healthy with your face bronzed by the sun.

Mathieu What's it like in Algeria?

Aziz I can't remember.

Mathieu Try. Make an effort.

Aziz Even when I try, I can't remember a thing.

Mathieu Why do you think of nothing but money, Aziz? All you ever do is work, work to pile up money. Stop working, Aziz; I'm talking to you.

Aziz   It's because I have need of money, and I only get money by working, and your father pays badly, so I can't afford to stop working.

Mathieu   I will tell him to pay you better. So what's war like, Aziz?

Aziz   I don't know. I've never known, and I don't want to know.

Mathieu   I don't want to know, either.

Aziz   Poor old Mathieu, don't be so sad. We'll go down to Saïfi's café tonight to drown your sorrows.

Mathieu   I don't want to drown my sorrows. And death, what's that like?

Aziz   How am I supposed to know? No more need of money, no need for a bed to lie down, no need to work at all, no more suffering, I suppose. I suppose it's not too bad.

Mathieu   I don't want to die.

Aziz   You'll be a hero, Mathieu. The French think their nation is made up of forty-five million heroes; why should you be any different? You're no more of an idiot than any other Frenchman. You'll come back all right; you'll have children double quick so as to tell them stories about your war. And if you don't come back they'll tell stories anyway, to other people's children.

Mathieu   I don't want to suffer.

Aziz   Wipe your face, now, here comes Maame Queuleu, she might think you were crying.

Mathieu   But I am crying, Aziz, I am crying.

Enter **Maame Queuleu**.

Maame Queuleu   Are you crying, Mathieu?

Mathieu   You must be joking, Maame Queuleu; I have never cried in my life and I don't intend to start today! (*Exit.*)

Maame Queuleu   I like it when the house is shrouded in sorrow. Mathilde is having a sulk with the master in the drawing room, Mathieu is crying, Fatima is groaning and complaining of the cold, Edouard is buried in his books, and everything is calm and silent and sad. The house is ours.

Scene 14

Distant bell ringing for Compline.

Mathilde (*to the audience*)   I never speak in the evening for the good reason that evenings are for falsehood. Outward agitation is a sign of inner tranquillity of spirit but the outward calm of a house is treacherous, hiding inner spiritual violence. That's why I don't speak in the evening, for the good reason that I, too, am a liar, I always have been and have every intention of going on being a liar. There is so little to distinguish, don't you think, between a yes and a no; it makes no difference which you use. So, what with the evening and me, things are bad, because, you see, two liars cancel each other out, and setting one falsehood against another, the truth begins to emerge. I detest the truth. That is why I avoid speaking in the evening; at all events, I try, for it is true that I am also something of a blabbermouth.

The real trial of our lives is our children; they get themselves conceived without asking anyone, and then there they are, thwarting you all through your life, calmly waiting to enjoy all the happiness that you've spent your life working to achieve, and only too pleased if you don't have the time to enjoy it yourself. All inheritance should be abolished: that's what destroys these provincial towns. The whole system of reproduction should be changed: women should give birth to stones. A stone doesn't thwart anyone: you just pick it up carefully, put it in a corner of the garden and forget about it. The stones should give birth to trees, the trees to birds and the birds to ponds.

From the ponds would come wolves and the wolves would give birth to human babies and suckle them. I wasn't made to be a woman. If only I'd been Adrien's brother, we could have had a manly friendship, we'd have gone pub crawling, had strong-arm competitions, swapped salacious stories in the dark, and now and then we'd have beaten one another senseless. But I wasn't made to be a man, either; perhaps even less. They are such arseholes. Fatima's right. Except she's not really right. When men get together they're able to be mates, when they get on well they're nice to each other, they don't complicate things. Actually, it's because they're so stupid that they don't complicate things, it doesn't occur to them, they lack something in the top storey by comparison with us. Whereas women friends are quite happy to make life difficult for one another; they like you, and just because they like you they do you all the harm they possibly can. It's because they have a few extra storeys up top.

Never tell a man you need him or you miss him or you love him because then he'll immediately think he's home and dry, that he can start to wear the trousers. He'll imagine he can hold the reins and play the clever-dick. You must never say anything, nothing at all, except in anger, when you can let any old thing pour out. But when it's not in anger, like now, and unless you're a real blabbermouth, it's best to say nothing.

In any case, Adrien will come with me when I leave, that is clear in my mind; I wanted him so I shall have him. I came without him, I shall leave with him. But silence, Mathilde, no more falsehood. The evening gives you the lie.

V

Scene 15

Saïfi's café.

Saïfi

عَزِيزْ فِيسَعْ ، هَاتْ اصْحَابَكْ ... قُلْهُمْ يخَلّصُوا غَادِي نْبَلّعْ الحَانُوتْ .

Aziz مَازَالْ صِيفِي . عْلاَشْ زَرْبَانْ ؟

Saïfi I'm closing; pay me and leave.

Aziz Pay him.

Mathieu The dick-head can only think of money.

Aziz وَالوُ بَاسْ صِيفِي ؟

Saïfi قُلْتَلَكْ غَادِي نْبَلّعْ .

Shut up. I don't want any fuss. Pay me and hurry. Pay me.

عَزِيزْ ، مَاتْسَارَاشْ فِي هَادِ السَّاعَةْ . كَايِنْ بالزَّافْ دِيَالْ رَاسِيسْتْ

They're coming to burn down my business. They've gone mad. Pay me.

عَزِيزْ ، عَزِيزْ عِنْدَكْ تُخْرُجْ مِنْ الدَّارْ . قُلْهُمْ يخَلّصُونِي نْدُوّحْ .

Aziz Pay him.

Mathieu The world's a mess. There's a price on every pleasure. I'm disgusted with pleasures.

Edouard Don't be upset Mathieu, it's only post-coital sadness.

Mathieu Why do the women throw themselves at you, Edouard? You're rickety, pimply, you look pathetic. Women are stupid prats, I shall never understand them.

Edouard You'll understand, you'll understand.

Saïfi There was someone who's not from the district; I

saw him hanging around the café several times, yesterday, the day before, and again today.

Edouard Perhaps he was here for the tarts.

Saïfi No, he didn't go off with a tart.

Mathieu He was visiting the district, going for a walk. Can't a person go for a walk in your district, Saïfi, without you getting frightened?

Saïfi People don't go walking in this district, and I didn't say I was frightened.

اصْحَابَكَ كَايِنْ يِزْعَقُوا عَلَيَّ . مَا نِبْغِيشْ نْعَاوِدْ نْشوُفْهُمْ .

Mathieu Stop talking that Arab bullshit.

Aziz كَانْ نْعَاهْدَكْ مَا نْعَاوِدْشْ نْجِيبْهُمْ .

Saïfi Pay me.

Mathieu Why do you ask me, Saïfi? There's three of us here: the rickety one, the Arab and me. Why is it always me who has to pay?

Aziz I'm not the Arab.

Saïfi أسْكُتْ عَزِيزْ

Edouard I'm not paying either.

Aziz I had to show you the way here.

Mathieu And I had to get you out of the house, Edouard, otherwise you'd still be tangled up in your stepmother's skirts.

Saïfi Piss off, piss off and don't pay me.

Mathieu If you aren't an Arab, what are you? A Frenchman? A servant? What should I call you?

Aziz A dick-head, I'm a dick-head. The only time anyone remembers my name is when they want to ask me for money. I spend my time like a fucking idiot in a house which isn't mine, digging a garden which isn't mine, scrubbing floors which aren't mine. And with the money that I earn I pay taxes to the French so that they can go to war against the Front and I pay taxes to the Front so that they can go to war on France. Meantime, who looks after Aziz in all that? No one. Who goes to war on Aziz? Everyone.

Saïfi Don't talk like that, Aziz.

Aziz The Front says I'm an Arab, the master says I'm a servant, the military say I'm French, and I say I'm a fucking idiot. Because I don't give a shit for the Arabs or the French or the master or the servants. I don't give a shit for Algeria or for France, for which side I'm supposed to be on, or not supposed to be on. I'm not for anyone and I'm not against anyone. And if they say I'm against them 'cos I'm not for them, then I'm against everything. I'm just a fucking dick-head idiot.

Mathieu He's drunk.

Edouard It's Ramadan getting to him.

Saïfi ‏إِنْتَ غَيْر نْزَايْرِي عَزِيز ..‏

Aziz ‏رَانِي مَا عْرِفْتْ حَاجَة صِيفِي ، وَاللَّه مَا عْرِفْتْ حَاجَة ..‏

Edouard Let's split. (*They move off, supporting* **Aziz**.)

Exit **Saïfi**. *The lights go down.*

Scene 16

Garden.
Enter **Adrien, Plantières, Borny**.

Adrien Not so much noise, Borny.

Borny It's Plantières: he's sticking so close to me that he made me trip.

Plantières I'm afraid you might disappear into the darkness.

Borny Plantières, I'll, I'll . . .

Plantières Go on then.

Adrien   Quiet! But wait a minute, where's Sablon? Where's he gone? When did we lose him?

Borny   There you are, Plantières: you see it's Sablon who's sidled off. Ha ha. There you are sticking to me like a limpet and meanwhile it's Sablon who disappears. He's off in his country retreat leaving us alone to face the fire, on hot coals, manning the front line. Ha ha Plantières, very clever, I must say.

Adrien   Shut up, here comes the girl.

They hide in the bushes.

Enter **Fatima**, *followed by* **Mathilde**.

Mathilde   Stop this idiocy, Fatima. Don't imagine that I believed it for a single instant. Foolishness, idiocy, religious mania. Whoever heard of apparitions these days? It was all very well for hysterical peasants in the countryside in the olden days. But today, it's quite grotesque. Even the blessed Virgin wouldn't dare. And you really thought I believed you? Beware, Fatima, beware; your uncle is only waiting for the slightest show of madness to do you harm.

Adrien   She's clever, my little sister.

Fatima   There she is: the cold and the light behind the walnut tree. Marie.

Explosion of **Saïfi**'s *café in the distance.*

Plantières   It's the café.

Borny   Now we're compromised.

Plantières   Shut your face, Borny.

Marie *appears.*

Adrien   Look at her: she's mad, she's mad.

Fatima   Marie, Marie, show yourself to the others; they don't believe me.

Marie   And why should I show myself to the others, little fool?

Fatima Because, because . . .

Marie Be quiet. I know them all inside out: Borny, Plantières, jumped-up officials, sons of peasants, gang of thugs disguised as bourgeois. Don't you think I've had my fill of those upstarts?

Fatima At least show yourself to Maman.

Marie Wouldn't dream of it: she's a fool.

Fatima Show yourself to my uncle, then, so that he won't torment me.

Marie But he will; he tormented me, and he'll do the same to you. Wealth doesn't change a man. That same Adrien, hiding in the bushes behind you, crawled out of the dirt and his feet still stink of it. What do you think his grandfather was? A miner, you little fool, a pit worker, black from morning to night, filthy even in his wedding bed. And his father? He was a miner too and his money didn't stop him being foul till the day of his death. Shame on me for marrying beneath myself into this disgusting family. I cannot forgive myself for it. I shall never forgive myself. We came from the real upper crust of this town; none of the Rozérieulles ever dirtied his hands. But every one of those men over there in the bushes stinks of the great unwashed and the *nouveaux riches*. And you're no better than them.

Plantières There's nothing there.

Adrien The girl, look at the way the girl's twitching.

Marie Tell your mother from me that she's a fool. She's a fool to have taken the smaller share of the inheritance, and she chose it herself. She chose this ridiculous house rather than the factory. Since she was common, she might at least have been rich. Now she's nothing, less than nothing. All I feel for her is shame. At least I retained some of the dignity of my class; no amount of money could have robbed me of that.

Fatima Aunt Marie, how did you die?

Plantières   The girl's mad, no doubt about it. But where's Sablon got to? He must section her.

Marie   Do you realise the humiliation I had to suffer from your uncle? The first time he invited me back to his parents' house, his mother had cooked some kind of pudding, a workman's cake made from the apples they had in the garden and some sort of coarse flour, margarine too, no doubt, or perhaps lard. I was ready for anything – determined not to pull a face and prepared to make a show of swallowing. But do you know what she did? I still bear the shame of it and it keeps me from finding peace.

Fatima   How did you die?

Marie   Her cake, her horrible cake, she presented it to me, oh! you'll never guess: she presented it to me, to *me* on a piece of newspaper. I wasn't expecting porcelain or crystal, I knew where I was. But newspaper! I will never forgive them for that.

Mathilde (*to* **Fatima**)   Stop pretending you're in a trance. What books have you been reading lately to put you in such a state?

Enter **Sablon**, *supporting* **Mathieu** *and* **Edouard**.

Sablon   Serpenoise, Serpenoise, look what I found, staggering in my headlights, bleeding and drunk, coming for Saïfi's café just after the bomb went off.

Adrien *goes up to* **Mathieu** *and slaps his face.*

Mathieu   Why should I be slapped, can't you see I'm bleeding?

Adrien (*slaps him again*)   Here's another to cancel out the first. It's in the Bible.

Fatima   Marie, how did you die? Maman wants to know.

Marie   I'm going, I must hurry. Do you think this is the only thing I have to do? (*She disappears.*)

Enter **Marthe**.

Marthe An apparition, they said there was an apparition here!

Mathilde The woman is dead drunk again.

Adrien Well, Sablon, you saw the girl, she's mad.

Mathilde My daughter is having a bad fit of depression, that's all. This rotten town would cause depression in a block of stone.

Marthe No, it's an apparition, I'm sure of it. Only the innocent have eyes to see it. It was the same at La Salette, rue du Bac, Mount Tepeyac, everywhere. Mama Rosa, Mama Rosa, there's a saint in my garden.

Exit **Edouard** *and* **Fatima**.

Sablon As for your servant, Adrien . . .

Adrien Well?

Sablon Stone dead.

Adrien Poor Aziz.

Sablon What the hell was your boy doing at Saïfi's café?

Plantières Ah if only we had known, you poor fool Adrien! Your own son! At our hands! But what was he doing there?

Borny If we'd only known . . .

Adrien But I knew perfectly well, my poor friends, I knew.

Exeunt.

Scene 17: Concerning very restricted relativity

Edouard (*to the audience*) If we are to believe the ancient authorities, and if they were not more mistaken than is reasonable to suppose; if we are to understand a part of the theories of modern science, which are much more complicated; in short, if I accept the findings of the scientists as correct, or more or less correct, and if they contain even a small part of the truth, and if I can believe them, even without understanding their process of reasoning, I arrive at the following conclusion: if the Earth is really round and its circumference is indeed forty thousand and seventy-four kilometres, if it really rotates on its axis every twenty-three hours, fifty-six minutes, as is claimed, then I am moving, at this very moment, in an easterly direction at a speed of one thousand, six hundred and seventy-nearly-two kilometres per hour. But I seem to be firmly fixed on the ground. Now, it is claimed – they claim, and I claim to believe them – that the Earth completes one revolution round the Sun every three hundred and sixty-five point two five days, describing a trajectory of nine hundred and forty million, four hundred and sixty-nine thousand, three hundred and seventy kilometres, which makes a speed of two million, five hundred and seventy-four thousand, eight hundred and sixty-three kilometres per hour, which should be added to the previous figure. So it seems that I am moving, right now, and without even making an effort, at a speed of two million, five hundred and seventy-six thousand, five hundred and thirty-four kilometres per hour. I'm inclined to believe it. I have no proof, unless it be my unshakeable faith in the Ancients, even though I don't entirely understand them, but I believe in them, and in the Moderns as well. So, provided I haven't overlooked some rule, and so long as some major law hasn't escaped me, given the facts, if I were to jump into the air and the Earth were to continue on its course through space, if I jump into the air and stay there for just two seconds, I should land up, when I fall back, one thousand four hundred kilometres from here, out in space; the Earth will be racing away from me at a dizzying speed, it will have escaped me and I shall have escaped from the Earth. There's no reason why it shouldn't work; the calculations are correct, the scientists are right. The one thing that worries me is that nobody, as far as I know, has thought of trying it out before me. Perhaps they were too attached to the Earth; of course nobody wants to end up heaven knows where, out in space; perhaps the inhabitants of this planet hold onto it with their hands, their toenails, their teeth, so as not to let go, and so that it doesn't let them go. They think their link with the planet is indissoluble, just as the leech probably thinks it's the skin that's holding it, whereas if it relaxed its jaws everything would separate and fly apart in space, each in its own direction. I should like the Earth to be going even faster; it seems a bit feeble, a bit slow, it lacks energy. But I suppose it's just a beginning; when I'm a few million kilometres from here, up in the air, things will be better. So I'm slipping away. I hope I'm not setting a bad example. It would be a disaster if the planet was deserted and even more of a disaster if space became full of people. In any case, here goes; I've nothing to lose. Two seconds in the air and everything'll be fine. I think it'll work. I believe the scientists, I have faith in them. I hope there isn't some law I've overlooked. Let's see.

He takes a run, jumps, and disappears into space.

Scene 18: Al-'îd ac-çaghîr

Mathilde   Are you putting your shoes on Adrien?

Adrien   You have set everyone in this town against me, I have no more friends, my son is half dead; I have nothing left to do here.

Mathilde   Quarrelling with one's friends is very good; it's something that should be done every seven years. You can't spend your whole life with your school friends. And where are you going?

Adrien   To Algeria.

Mathilde   Algeria? You're mad.

Adrien   Well you went there didn't you? Where do you suggest I go? I don't know anywhere else, apart from here. I've never been away. Even for my military service I stayed here, because of my flat feet, and I came home every evening.

Mathilde   There's Andorra, Monaco, Geneva; paradise havens for the rich, the only places in the world where it's really worth living. In places like that all your neighbours are rich, wars never touch you and there are no children, or at least they are kept behind railings by nursemaids. You are surrounded by people who are perfectly sterile, old, satisfied, where there's nobody to annoy you. Why does everyone long to be young? It's idiotic.

Adrien   That's all very well, but it sounds expensive. The factory's not worth that much and I fear I won't get a good price for it. Because of you, I've let it go: you owe me compensation, Mathilde. Pay me back, Mathilde, pay me for that and for all the improvements I've made to this house, and I'll clear off to Tahiti.

Mathilde   You're insane, Adrien. Not a penny. Just go to Algeria. It's lovely there.

Adrien   Why did you leave then, if it's so lovely? Just to annoy me?

Mathilde   I was bored. When it's lovely I get bored. The world I know isn't lovely.

Adrien   Wasn't there a war, or something like that?

Mathilde   Why are you going on about a war when I'm talking about things that are important?

Enter **Maame Queuleu**.

Maame Queuleu   Madame, Madame, your daughter Fatima has just been taken sick. She fell to the ground like a tree torn up by a typhoon. She's groaning and twisting and she won't let us touch her.

Adrien   Loosen her collar; take that absurd bundle of clothes off her. Anyone would feel ill wrapped up like that in the middle of summer.

Maame Queuleu   She says no, sir, she says she's cold.

She's shivering and her teeth are chattering, and she says no.

Mathilde   Force her.

Exit **Maame Queuleu**.

Adrien   So, you were bored in Algeria, were you, Mathilde?

Mathilde   Yes, I was bored.

Adrien   Because you missed me?

Mathilde   I was bored, Adrien.

Adrien   I was bored too.

Mathilde   But you chose to stay here. Why should you be bored?

Adrien   I was bored here.

Mathilde   You had your son.

Adrien   What difference does that make? I was bored, here, with my son.

Enter **Maame Queuleu**.

Maame Queuleu   Madame, Madame, what a misfortune!

Mathilde   What is it now?

Maame Queuleu   Your daughter was pregnant, Madame, and now she's giving birth. What should I do? What should I do?

Mathilde   Well, see to her, pull it out, cut the cord. You know how to do all that, don't you?

Exit **Maame Queuleu**.

Adrien   Well, well; despite her air of innocence, Fatima knows a thing or two.

Mathilde   No need to know anything, Adrien.

Adrien   You're well placed to judge, dear sister.

Mathilde   Shut your mouth. I'm nobody's fool. Adrien,

you can't leave. There's your wife, your woman, your concubine. Poor Marthe, she could never manage on her own. Besides, I believe she loves you. It's not that easy to get rid of a wife who loves you.

Adrien   Maame Queuleu will see to her. In any case, see if I care; I'm not going to spend my life nursing a drunkard.

Mathilde   Poor Marthe! Men really are pigs.

Adrien   In the meantime your daughter – what's her name again? Caroline? – she's the one who'll inherit the house. Your daughter is a crafty little devil.

Mathilde   Women can put up with misfortune better, that's all.

Adrien   Other people's misfortune, yes, that's right: they flourish on the misfortunes of others. In fact you're beginning to look quite pretty yourself, Mathilde my little sister.

Mathilde   In any case, she won't inherit a thing. I'm selling up this old pile and I'm off.

Adrien   And where to, little sister?

Mathilde   What difference can it make to you, brother Adrien, what difference can it make? Tell me, Adrien.

Adrien   Yes?

Mathilde   Am I really as pretty as you said? Still pretty, I mean? Still a bit pretty, at least?

Adrien   You are, Mathilde, you are.

Enter **Maame Queuleu**.

Mathilde   What fresh misfortune have you got for us, Maame Queuleu? You look fit to wither the leaves on the trees.

Maame Queuleu   Ah, Madame, Master.

Adrien   Well go on. Won't it come out? Can't you manage? Should I call a doctor?

Maame Queuleu   Too late, sir. It all passed off well.

Adrien   So?

Mathilde   Is it dead?

Maame Queuleu   Oh no, Madame, on the contrary.

Mathilde   How do you mean, on the contrary? It's alive, then?

Maame Queuleu   They are alive, Madame, they are alive: there's two of them. And just before she passed out she baptised them with two foreign names.

Adrien   What names? What names?

Maame Queuleu   Remus, I think, and the other was Romulus.

Mathilde   Adrien, you're annoying me again. The minute I decide to go, to leave this town, to sell up and clear out, you have to decide to do the same. Of course, I am the eldest, but I'm fed up with the way you copy everything I do.

Adrien   Excuse me, Mathilde, excuse me: I was already getting my shoes on and your bags aren't even packed; I told you I was leaving before you even started talking about it. Me? Imitate you? I'm not stupid. I've always behaved well and I've never approved of your way of carrying on. I've always been on the side of good manners, on Father's side.

Mathilde   That's right, on Father's side and against me. You copied him, you were his poodle. You approved of his making me eat on my knees, and you sneered at me while I did it.

Adrien   I did not sneer, Mathilde, I swear to you that it was an expression of pain.

Mathilde   And now that Father's dead, you want to imitate me. Well it's not on. I'm not your daddy.

Adrien   If I decide to sell up and leave, that's what I shall do.

Mathilde   All right then, so shall I. I see no reason why I shouldn't.

Adrien   You'll get a tidy sum from this house, little sister.

Mathilde   As you will from your factory, little brother.

Adrien   Not all that much, not all that much.

Mathilde   It won't be all that much for me, either.

Adrien   You're already beginning to fiddle the accounts.

Mathilde   I'm doing no such thing. I'm quite open, Adrien, always have been.

Adrien   Well Maame Queuleu? Eavesdropping?

Mathilde   What are you doing there? Are you growing roots?

Adrien   Speak up or get out.

Maame Queuleu   Well, it's . . .

Mathilde   Are they damaged? Blind? Deformed? Are they stuck together?

Maame Queuleu   Oh no Madame, on the contrary.

Mathilde   So they're all right?

Maame Queuleu   Alas, they're perfect, Madame, big, strong, lusty, bright-eyed. Alas, they're beautiful.

Mathilde   Well, why are you so sorry for yourself?

Maame Queuleu   I'm not sorry for myself, Madame, I'm not. It's you I'm sorry for.

Mathilde   Oh yes? Me? And what, pray, is going to happen to me?

Adrien   Speak up, Maame Queuleu, or I shall beat you.

Maame Queuleu   The thing is, sir, they're . . .

Mathilde   Yes?

Adrien   Well?

Maame Queuleu They're . . . they're . . .

Adrien Spit it out, in God's name.

Maame Queuleu Black, sir, they're black as black, with crinkly hair.

Exit crying.

Mathilde Hurry up, Adrien, for heaven's sake, hurry. It takes you an age to tie your shoes.

Adrien What about your bags, Mathilde?

Mathilde They're ready, you poor old thing, I never unpacked. Now hurry up.

Adrien I'm coming, I'm coming. But what's the hurry, little sister.

Mathilde I have no desire to see the children of my daughter grow up. Those two will create havoc in this town, and it won't take long.

Adrien I thought that was what you came back to do, Mathilde.

Mathilde Too late for me, little brother; I shall have to be satisfied with getting at you.

Adrien Don't begin again, Mathilde, please don't.

Mathilde Do you call this a beginning, Adrien?

Exeunt.

Translations of passages in Arabic

Scene 1

Aziz It looks like it's going to be a filthy day.

Mathilde And why should it be a filthy day?

Aziz Because if the sister is as big an arsehole as the brother, things don't look good.

Mathilde The sister is not as big an arsehole as the brother.

Aziz And how come you know that?

Mathilde Because I am the sister.

Scene 15

Saïfi Aziz, hurry up, you and your friends must leave; tell them to pay and I'm shutting up shop.

Aziz It's not time yet, Saïfi; why are you in such a hurry?

[. . .]

Aziz What's the matter, Saïfi?

Saïfi I have to close, I tell you. [. . .] Aziz, don't hang about in the street tonight. There are fascist gangs about. [. . .] Aziz, Aziz, don't leave home again. Tell them to pay me and get out.

[. . .]

Saïfi Your friends are a pain in the arse, Aziz, I don't want to see them again.

[. . .]

Aziz I won't bring them back, I promise you.

[. . .]

Saïfi Shut up, Aziz.

[. . .]

Saïfi   You're an Algerian, Aziz, and that's an end of it.

Aziz   I don't know, Saïfi, I don't know anything.

The five daily prayers of the Islamic religion are, in the following succession: *sobh* (dawn), *zohr* (towards midday), *'açr* (afternoon), *maghrib* (evening), and *'ichâ* (night). *Al-'îd ac-çaghîr* is the name of the festival marking the end of Ramadan.

OAS stood for *Organisation de l'Armèe Secrète*, a secret faction of army officers dedicated to retaining France's colonial presence in Algeria. The acronym OAS also stood for the fictional title, *Office d'Action Sociale*, used by OAS sympathisers as a front for collecting funds in support of the officers. (See Scene 5.)

Roberto Zucco

translated by MARTIN CRIMP

Characters

Roberto Zucco
His mother
A girl
Her sister
Her brother
Her father
Her mother
An old gentleman
An elegant lady
Bruiser
Impatient pimp
Panic-stricken prostitute
Melancholy detective
A police superintendent
A police sergeant
First prison officer
Second prison officer
First police officer
Second police officer
Men. Women. Prostitutes. Pimps. The voices of prisoners and prison officers

[*Translator's note*: In his crowd scenes, i.e. 8, 10 and 15, Koltès does not number or distinguish the speakers.]

After the second prayer you will see how the disc of the sun unfolds, and you will see hanging down from it the phallus, the origin of the wind, and when you move your face to the regions of the east it will move there, and if you move your face to the regions of the west it will follow you.

Mithras Liturgy, part of the Great Parisian Magic Papyrus. (Quoted by Carl Jung in his last interview for the BBC.)

Scene 1: Break-out

A prison surveillance post at roof level.
Prison rooftops visible.
*The time of night when prison officers, because of the silence
and strain of staring into the dark, occasionally succumb to
hallucinations.*

1st Officer You hear a noise?

2nd Officer Noise? What noise?

1st Officer You never hear noises, do you?

2nd Officer Are you saying you heard a noise?

1st Officer I'm saying I think it's a possibility.

2nd Officer Well, did you or didn't you?

1st Officer Maybe not with my actual ears, but
potentially – yes I did.

2nd Officer Potentially but not with your actual *ears*?

1st Officer You see, the reason you never hear or see
anything is because you lack the potential.

2nd Officer The reason I never hear or see anything is
because there's never anything to see or hear. We don't
have a *raison d'être*, and it's because we don't have a *raison
d'être* that we always end up fucking arguing. Guns,
alarms that never go off, eyes wide open when everyone
else has theirs tight shut – and no *raison de* fucking *être*.
And it seems pointless to be staring into space or listening
out for non-existent sounds when our ears could be tuned
into our own inner worlds and our eyes could be
contemplating our own inner landscapes. D'you believe
in the inner world?

1st Officer I believe we have a *raison d'être* which is to
prevent escapes.

2nd Officer   But this is a modern prison. Escape is not possible. Escape is not an inmate option. Not even for a tiny tiny one. Not even for a rat-sized one. Even if the bastard got through the bars he'd still have to get through the mesh. And even if he got through the mesh he'd still have to get through the membrane after the mesh – run through it like a liquid. And there's nothing liquid about the arm of a strangler or the hand that's stabbed a man. They're all too solid flesh, believe you me. What d'you think makes someone a potential killer? I mean not just potential but actually do it.

1st Officer   Sheer evil.

2nd Officer   Because I've been a prison officer for six years now, and whenever I look at a killer I ask myself what makes him different – what makes him different from a prison officer like myself who couldn't stab or strangle *any*one – not even *potentially*. I've thought and thought about this and even watched them in the showers after someone told me the killer instinct is located in a man's penis. I've seen over six hundred of them, and the fact is no two are the same – big ones, small ones, tiny tiny ones, rounded ones, pointy ones, great fat thick ones, but nothing conclusive.

1st Officer   I'm telling you: it's sheer evil. Are you sure you can't see something?

Zucco *appears, walking along the ridge of the roof.*

2nd Officer   No. Nothing.

1st Officer   Neither can I – but I'm talking about *potentially*.

2nd Officer   You don't mean that bastard walking on the roof? That's a hallucination due to lack of sleep.

1st Officer   Why should some bastard be walking on the roof anyway? You were right. There are times when we should completely close our eyes on the inner world.

2nd Officer   He even looks a bit like Roberto Zucco, the

one they sent down this afternoon for killing his own
father. Wild violent animal bastard.

1st Officer   Roberto Zucco. Never heard of him.

2nd Officer   Seriously. Can you see something? Or is it
just me?

Zucco *continues to move unhurriedly along the roof.*

1st Officer   Potentially I see something. The question is
what?

Zucco *begins to vanish behind a chimney.*

2nd Officer   An inmate escaping.

Zucco *has vanished.*

1st Officer   Fuck it. You're right. It's a break-out.

Gunfire, searchlights, sirens.

Scene 2: He murders his mother

Zucco's **Mother** *in her nightdress in front of the locked
door.*

Mother   My hand's on the phone, Roberto. I'm picking
it up and I'm calling the police.

Zucco   Let me in.

Mother   Go away.

Zucco   Do I have to kick the door down? Well? Don't be
so stupid.

Mother   Go on then. *Kick* it down. Wake up the
neighbours. You're sick in the head, Roberto. You were
better off in prison. If they see you here they'll take the
law into their own hands. Because a boy doesn't kill his
own father. Not in this neighbourhood. Even the dogs
despise you.

Zucco *bangs on the door.*

Mother How did you get out anyway? What kind of prison do they call that?

Zucco No one will ever keep me in a prison for more than a few hours. No one. Let me in. You'd try the patience of a *snail*. Let me in or I'll smash the whole fucking place up.

Mother What d'you think you're doing coming back here? I don't want to see your face ever again. Understand? You're not my son any more – you're just a fly buzzing round shit.

Zucco *smashes the door down.*

Mother Don't touch me, Roberto.

Zucco I want my fatigues.

Mother Your what?

Zucco Fatigues. The khaki shirt and the combat trousers.

Mother You mean that stupid soldier-suit? What d'you need a stupid soldier-suit for? You're mad, Roberto. If only we'd realised when you were a baby and put you out for the bin-men.

Zucco Hurry up. Come on. I need it now.

Mother I'll give you money. Money's what you need. Then you can buy all the stupid soldier-suits you want.

Zucco I don't want money. I want my fatigues.

Mother Over my dead body, Roberto. I'm calling the neighbours.

Zucco I want my fatigues.

Mother Don't shout at me, Roberto. Don't shout. You're frightening me. Don't shout or you'll wake the neighbours up. I can't give you those clothes. They're revolting. They're not clean. You can't go out dressed like that. At least let me wash and dry them and put a nice crease in the trousers.

Zucco   I can do all that myself in the launderette.

Mother   The launderette? You must be out of your tiny little mind.

Zucco   I love launderettes. Calm. Peaceful. And full of women.

Mother   I don't give a damn. You're not having them. Don't touch me, Roberto. I'm still in mourning for your father – are you going to kill me too?

Zucco   Come on Mum, don't be frightened. I've always been nice and kind to you, haven't I? Why be afraid? Why not just give me my fatigues? I need them, Mum, I really need them.

Mother   I don't want you to be nice to me, Roberto. Do you really expect me to forget that you killed your own father? That you tossed him out of that window the way other people toss a cigarette? And then you start being nice to me? I don't want to forget you killed your father, Roberto – and if you're nice to me, I'll forget everything.

Zucco   That's right. Forget. Give me my fatigues. The khaki shirt and the combat trousers. Clean or not. Pressed or not. Give them to me. And then I promise you I'll go.

Mother   I can't believe I gave birth to you, Roberto. I can't believe you were ever inside of me. If it hadn't been in this room, if I hadn't seen you come out of my body and watched you being laid in the cot – if I hadn't seen you with my own eyes growing and changing, watching you so closely that I didn't even notice the changes happening – and if you suddenly appeared and said you were the son I gave birth to in this bed, I'd refuse to believe you. But I recognise you, Roberto. I recognise you only too well – the size and the shape of your body – the colour of your hair and of your eyes – the shape of your hands – those huge strong hands of yours which you've only ever used to stroke your mother's neck – and break your father's – and murder him. What makes a boy who's been so good for twenty-four years suddenly go insane?

What makes him leave the rails, Roberto? Who put the
tree across the straight and narrow track and forced you
over the edge? Roberto, Roberto, when a car is wrecked at
the bottom of the ravine you don't repair it. When a train
goes off the rails you don't try and put it back on the
tracks. You leave it. You forget it. And I'll forget you,
Roberto. You're already forgotten.

Zucco   Before you forget me completely, you can tell me
where my fatigues are.

Mother   Screwed up in the basket. I told you: they're
filthy. (**Zucco** *gets them out.*) Now get out like you
promised.

Zucco   Yes. Like I promised.

*He goes up to her, strokes her, kisses her, grips her. She
moans.*
When he lets go she drops to the floor, strangled.
Zucco *undresses, slips on the fatigues and goes.*

Scene 3: Under the table

A kitchen.
A table covered with a cloth reaching to the ground.
The **Girl**'s **Sister** *appears.*
She goes to the window and opens it part way.

Sister   Inside. Quietly. Shoes off. Sit down and shut up.

The **Girl** *climbs in through the window.*

Sister   And so, in the middle of the night, I finally
discover you squatting against the wall. Your brother's
taken the car. He's searching the whole city. He's gone
completely out of his mind. And believe you me he'll have
more than your pants down when he finds you. Your
mother's been glued to the window for hours imagining
everything imaginable from gang-rape by a bunch of
thugs to finding your dismembered body in the woods –
not to mention being trapped in the cellar by a

psychopath – you name it. Your father's so convinced
he'll never see you again he's got himself totally pissed
and now he's snoring in desperation on the sofa. And here
am I, here am I running round like an idiot while all the
time you're squatting there against the wall. Why
couldn't you just've crossed the yard and set our minds at
rest? What did you hope to achieve? Because believe you
me he'll have your pants down. And I hope he makes you
bleed.

Pause.

So, I see you've decided not to talk to me. You've decided
silence is more dramatic. Silence. Silence. Silence. Panic
all around but I'm not telling. My lips are sealed. Well
we'll see just how sealed they really are when your brother
gets your pants down. Open that little mouth of yours and
explain to me why you were back so late when you were
told midnight. Because if you don't open that little mouth
I'm going to start panicking, I'm going to start imagining
things, just like the others. Come on, my baby robin. Tell
your sister. You know I always understand. And if he's
violent, I promise I'll protect you.

Pause.

It's a boy, isn't it. You've been out with some boy. Some
typical idiot boy. What did he do? Fumble about? Grope
you about? We've all been there, my little lovebird. We've
all been babies. We've all been to parties with those idiot
boys. Getting kissed can't hurt you. You'll get kissed by
plenty of idiot boys whether you like it or not. You'll get
their idiot hands up your skirt whether you want it or not.
Because boys have no brains and putting their hands up a
girl's skirt is the best they can manage. They absolutely
love it. I don't know what they get out of it. Nothing at all
if you ask me. It's just what they do. They can't help
themselves. They were born like that – mentally
defective. But it's not worth *worrying* about. All that
matters is that they don't take from you the thing which
must not be taken. Because there's a time and a place for

that, as well you know. And your mother, and father, and brother, myself, and you too, will make that decision. Unless someone's used force. And who'd dare to use force on a pure innocent child? Well? Tell me no one has used force. Tell me, please tell me no one has taken the thing which must not be taken. Talk to me. Talk to me or I'm going to get very angry. (*A noise.*) Quickly. Under the table. It sounds like your brother.

The **Girl** *disappears under the table.*

Their **Father** *enters, half asleep, in his pyjamas. He goes through the kitchen, vanishes for a moment, reappears and goes back to his room.*

Sister   You're still a child. You're still a virgin. You still belong to your sister, to your brother, to your father and to your mother. I don't want to hear this. It's horrible. Shut up. I'm going mad. You've thrown yourself away, and dragged the rest of us with you.

Their **Brother** *comes crashing in. The* **Sister** *throws herself at him.*

Sister   Calm down and don't start shouting. She's not here but she has been found. She has been found but she isn't here. Calm down or I'll go mad. Don't make things worse by shouting or I'll kill myself.

Brother   Where is she? *Tell* me.

Sister   At a friend's. Sleeping at a friend's. Warm and safe in her friend's bed. Nothing – believe me – can hurt her. But something – yes – evil has happened. Don't start shouting. Please. You know you'll regret it. You know there'll be tears.

Brother   There'll only be tears if something evil has happened to my baby sister. I've kept such a close eye on her and this is the only night she's got away – the only night she's got away from me in all these years. It takes more time than that for evil to destroy someone.

Sister   Evil doesn't take time. It comes when it wants

and in a moment it changes everything. In one moment it can smash the precious object you've spent – yes – years protecting.

She takes an object and drops it on the floor.

And it can't be mended. You can scream and you can shout, but it will never mend.

*Their **Father** enters. He crosses the room as before and disappears.*

Brother   Help me. Please. Help me. You're stronger than me. I can't deal with evil.

Sister   No one can deal with evil.

Brother   But you can help me.

Sister   Not deal with evil, no.

Brother   Christ, I need a drink. (*He goes out.*)

*Their **Father** reappears.*

Father   What's this then? Crying? Did I hear someone crying?

Sister *gets up.*

Sister   I was singing to myself, that's all. (*She goes out.*)

Father   So you should. It wards off evil. (*He goes out.*)

*A moment passes, then the **Girl** emerges from under the table, goes to the window and lets in **Zucco**.*

Girl   Take your shoes off. What's your name?

Zucco   Whatever you like. What's yours?

Girl   I don't have a name any more. Little this, little that – little robin, little lovebird, little cuckoo, little sparrow, little nightingale or skylark, little dove – that's all they ever call me. I'd prefer little pig, little rattlesnake or little rat. What do you do in real life?

Zucco   In real life?

Girl   Real life, yes – the things people do – get work, get jobs, get paid.

Zucco   I don't do the things people do.

Girl   Then what *do* you do?

Zucco   I'm a secret agent. D'you know what a secret agent is?

Girl   I know what a secret is.

Zucco   Secret agents aren't just secret. They travel. They go all over the world. And have guns.

Girl   Have you got a gun?

Zucco   Of course I've got a gun.

Girl   Show me then.

Zucco   Not allowed.

Girl   Then you're a liar.

Zucco   I've got this. (*Takes out knife.*)

Girl   That's not a gun.

Zucco   It's just as good for killing people.

Girl   What else do secret agents do, apart from kill people?

Zucco   Travel. Go to Africa. Have you been to Africa?

Girl   Of course.

Zucco   In Africa I've been to places where the mountains are so high it always snows. No one knows it snows in Africa. But it's the best thing in the world: African snow falling on the frozen African lakes.

Girl   I'd love to see African snow. I'd love to skate on the frozen lakes.

Zucco   And walking across the snow-covered lakes there are white rhinoceroses.

Girl   What's your name? Tell me.

Zucco   I won't ever tell you my name.

Girl   Why not? I want to know.

Zucco   Because it's a secret.

Girl   I can keep secrets. Go on. Tell me.

Zucco   Can't remember.

Girl   Liar.

Zucco   Andreas.

Girl   Liar.

Zucco   Angelo.

Girl   I'm going to scream if you make fun of me. It's not any of those stupid names.

Zucco   How d'you know that when you don't know what it is?

Girl   It can't be. I'd recognise it straight away.

Zucco   I'm not allowed to tell you.

Girl   Even if you're not allowed, tell me anyway.

Zucco   I can't. Something terrible could happen.

Girl   So what? Tell me anyway.

Zucco   If I told you, I'd die.

Girl   Tell me – even if you have to die.

Zucco   Roberto.

Girl   Roberto what?

Zucco   Come on. That's enough.

Girl   Roberto what? If you don't tell me I'll scream, and my brother who's very very angry will come and kill you.

Zucco   When you told me you knew what a secret was, did you really mean it?

Girl   It's the only thing I really do really know. Roberto what? Tell me.

Zucco   Zucco.

Girl   Roberto Zucco. I'll never forget that name. Hide under the table. Someone's coming.

Her **Mother** *enters.*

Mother   Talking to yourself, my little cuckoo?

Girl   Just singing to ward off evil.

Mother   So you should. (*Sees the broken object.*) Thank God. I never could stand the sight of that piece of shit.

Mother *goes out.*

The **Girl** *joins* **Zucco** *under the table.*

Girl's voice   Listen to me: you've taken my virginity, and it's yours to keep. No one else can take it from me now. You'll have it for the rest of your life, even when you've forgotten me, even when you're dead. I've marked you for life like a scar after a fight. And I can never forget, because it can't be given again. Not to anyone. It's finished. It's gone. Till the day I die. I've given it away and now it's yours.

Scene 4: The melancholy detective

Brothel reception in the neighbourhood known as 'Little Chicago'.

Detective   I'm not a happy man. I'm sick at heart and I just can't fathom it. I'm often unhappy but this time something jars. Usually when I feel like this and get the urge to weep or die, I try and find a reason. I go back over everything that's happened during the day, the night, the previous day – and I always end up discovering some insignificant event which – however meaningless at the time – has stuck in me like some bastard of a bug tearing my guts apart. And once I've identified the meaningless event giving me so much grief then I'm laughing. Bug eliminated – like a louse by a fingernail – end of story. But this time it's different. I've traced and retraced every step of the past three days only to end up back where I started: none the wiser, none the happier, and sick to the heart.

Madam   Too much tinkering with pimps and dead bodies, Detective Sergeant.

Detective   There are less dead bodies than people think. But yes – you're right – far too many pimps. My policy would be minimise pimps, maximise dead bodies.

Madam   Personally I prefer pimps. I'd rather make a living out of the living.

Detective   And I must be on my way. Goodbye.

Zucco *emerges from a room and locks the door.*

Madam   Never say goodbye, Sergeant.

The **Detective** *leaves, followed by* **Zucco**.

After a few moments a panic-stricken **Prostitute** *comes in.*

Prostitute   Oh God, oh God. The forces of darkness have just swept through the streets of Little Chicago. The neighbourhood's stunned. The girls can't work. The pimps can't speak. The clients have fled. Everything's stopped. Everything's paralysed. You've harboured a devil in this house. That boy who just came, who never opened his lips, who never answered the girls' questions, who seemed speechless, sexless, but had such a gentle face – rather good-looking actually and gave the girls a lot to talk about – you should've seen the way he followed the sergeant out. We're all watching him, having a laugh, making various suppositions. He's right behind the sergeant who seems deep in thought – right behind him like his shadow – and the shadow shrinking like in the midday sun. He's getting closer and closer to the sergeant's hunched body when suddenly he pulls a long knife out of his jacket pocket and stabs it into the poor man's back. The sergeant stops. Doesn't turn round. Gently nods his head as if the question he was pondering has at last been answered. Then his whole body sways,

and he collapses on the ground. Not for one moment has
the murderer seen the victim or the victim the murderer.
The boy's eyes are glued to the sergeant's gun. He bends
down, removes it, pockets it, and calmly continues on his
way, as calm as the Antichrist. And nobody moves.
Everyone just stands there watching him go, watching
him vanish into the crowd. It was the devil himself. And
he was in this house.

Madam   Devil or not, kill a policeman and the boy's as
good as fucked.

Scene 5: Brotherly love

Kitchen.
Girl *against the wall, in a state of terror.*

Brother   Don't be scared of me, my little lovebird. I'm
not going to hurt you. Your sister's an idiot. What made
her think I was going to hit you? You're cunt now. I never
hit cunt. I like cunt. Cunt's what I prefer. I certainly
prefer it to a baby sister. A baby sister's a pain. All that
attention. All that loving care. And to protect her what? –
her *virginity*? Because just how long are you supposed to
protect a girl's virginity? All that time I've spent on you is
now totally wasted. And I regret every moment. I regret
every wasted day and every wasted hour. Girls should be
fucked and off their big brothers' backs as soon as it's
physically possible. Then there'd be nothing left to
protect and we could spend our time on better things. So
I'm not complaining if you get yourself laid. In fact it's a
weight off my mind. It means we can go our separate ways
without you round my legs like a ball and fucking chain.
Tell you what: let's go and have a drink. It's time you
learned to stop blushing and staring at the floor because
that's all over now. Shock the bastards. Get your head up,
meet their eyes and stare them out. They love it. There's
no point holding yourself back now, sweetheart. Just go
for it. Fuck it. Do it. Hang out in Little Chicago with the

working girls. Get on the game. Earn some cash and some independence. And perhaps I'll meet you working the bars, and nod ever so slightly – out of brotherly love – and we'll have a fucking good brotherly sisterly time, eh? So don't waste your energy staring at the floor with your legs squeezed together, my little lovebird, because what is the point? I mean you can forget marriage. Yes it made sense saving you for a husband. Yes it made sense staring at the floor waiting for your wedding-day. But you can forget wedding-days now – and everything else for that matter. Marriage, family, father, mother, sister – all totally fucked in one fell swoop and I don't give a shit. Father snoring. Mother in tears. Far better leave them to their tears and misery and quit this house. Get pregnant if you like – who cares? Or not. Who gives a shit? Do just what you like. I'm not your guardian any more. You're not a child any more. Your age is irrelevant: fifteen or fifty, it's all the same. What you are is cunt. And no one gives a toss.

Scene 6: Metro

A wanted poster with an unnamed picture of **Zucco**.
Caption: 'Have you seen this man?'
Beneath it, side by side on a bench, an **Old Gentleman** *and*
Zucco.
The station has shut down for the night.

Old Gentleman   I'm an old man and it's not sensible for me to be out this late. I was still congratulating myself on having caught the last train when – come to a fork in this labyrinth of corridors and stairways – I suddenly realised I'd lost my bearings – even though I use this station so often that I thought I knew it like my own front door. I had no idea that beyond my tried and trusted everyday track there lurked a dark world of tunnels and unknown paths of which I would rather, quite frankly, have remained in ignorance, if my stupid absent-mindedness hadn't forced me to make their acquaintance.

Just like that the lights went out, leaving only these little
white lamps of whose existence I was utterly unaware,
and myself walking on and on as fast as I could through
an unfamiliar world – not that 'fast' means much when
you get to be my age. And just when at the end of endless
motionless escalators I thought I could see a way out –
crash! – down comes a vast metal shutter. So here I am, in
a rather peculiar situation for a man of my age, a victim of
absent-mindedness and a lack of agility, not quite sure
what I'm waiting for, and not quite sure quite frankly that
I want to be sure, since at my time of life new experiences
are not at all welcome. Dawn, I suppose. I suppose I'm
waiting for the dawn here in this station which seemed as
familiar as my own front door before it became so
frightening. I suppose I'm waiting for the lights to come
back on and for the trains to start. But what worries me is
how I'll ever see daylight again after this ludicrous
adventure? And the station will never be the same. I'll
always be aware of these little white lamps which
previously did not exist. And staying up through the
night – I've never done it before – who knows how one's
life could be altered? Everything must get out of step if
night doesn't follow day the way it used to. I find that all
very disturbing. But as for you, young man, who seem as
clear-headed as you are able-bodied – yes – whose clear
gaze is so obviously not the dull and foolish gaze of an old
man such as myself, it's impossible to believe that you
have let yourself be ensnared by all these corridors and
steel shutters. Surely a young clear-headed boy like you
could slip through the mesh like water through a sieve.
Do you work nights here? Tell me about yourself and set
my mind at rest.

Zucco   I'm just a normal sensible young man who never
draws attention to himself. Would you have even noticed
me if I wasn't sitting right next to you? I've always
thought that the best way to live in peace is to be as
transparent as a pane of glass, like a chameleon on a stone
– to walk through walls – to be colourless and odourless.

To let people see right through you to the people on the
other side, as if you just weren't there. It's no easy job to
be transparent. It takes dedication. To be invisible is an
old – an ancient dream. I'm not a hero. Heroes are
criminals. There's not one hero whose clothes aren't
drenched in blood – and blood is the one thing in the
world that never goes unnoticed. When the end finally
comes, and the earth is smothered by the smoke of
destruction, the blood-soaked rags of heroes will remain.
You're talking to a student – a good one. Learn to be a
good student and you never look back. I have a place at
university – on the ancient benches of the Sorbonne – a
seat reserved in the middle of all those other good
students who don't even notice me. Because believe you
me you need to be a good student – invisible and discreet
– to go to the Sorbonne. It's not one of these red-brick
places full of yobs who think they're heroes. Shadowy
figures pace the silent corridors and their footsteps make
no sound. Starting tomorrow I'm going back to pursue
linguistics. Tomorrow, you see, is linguistics day. And
there I'll be – an invisible man among invisible men –
silent and attentive behind the smokescreen of everyday
life. Nothing can change the course of things, nothing. I
calmly cross the prairie like a train that can never leave
the tracks. I'm like a hippopotamus moving very slowly
through the mud, whose chosen path and pace nothing
can alter.

Old Gentleman   You can always leave the tracks,
young man. Anyone – as I now know – can leave the
tracks at any moment. Even an old man, even a man who
thought he knew life and the world like his own front door
can be suddenly – crash! – shut out of the world. At this
nothing o'clock. In this unnatural light. Full of fear of
what may happen when the lights come back on and the
trains begin and the station fills with people as ordinary as
he once was. And after my first night without sleep I'll
have no choice but to go out past the now open shutters
and, without having witnessed the night, confront the

day. I've no idea what will happen. How will I see the
world? And how will the world see – or fail to see – me?
No longer able to distinguish day from night, I won't
know what to do. I'll be pacing up and down in my
kitchen searching for the right time and, quite frankly, it's
all making me rather afraid.

Zucco   Well you have every reason to be.

Old Gentleman   You have a very slight stammer,
which I find rather attractive and puts me at my ease.
When the chaos here begins, would you help me? Would
you? Would you help a lost old man like myself to the
exit? If not beyond?

The lights come back on.
Zucco *helps the* **Old Gentleman** *get up, and leads him
away as the first train passes.*

Scene 7: Two sisters

The kitchen.
The **Girl** *with a bag.*
Her **Sister** *appears.*

Sister   I forbid you to leave.

Girl   You have no right to. From now on I'm the oldest.

Sister   The oldest? You? You're just a baby robin
perched on a branch. *I'm* big sister.

Girl   More like professional virgin. You take such *care*
of yourself, you're so in *love* with yourself – what do you
know about life? *I* was raped, *I* was abandoned, *I'm* the
oldest, and I'll make my own decisions.

Sister   But you're the baby sister who told me all her
secrets!

Girl   And you're the one left on the shelf who knows
nothing about anything, has no experience and should
learn to keep her mouth shut!

Sister   Experience? A bad experience is no use to anyone. All you can do is try and forget it as quickly as possible. Only good experiences are worth having. You'll always remember the lovely quiet evenings you spent with your brother and sister and your parents – they'll stay with you even when you're old. Whereas you'll soon forget this tragedy of ours, my little cuckoo, under your brother and sister and parents' watchful eye.

Girl   Your 'watchful eye' is exactly what I want to forget – not my so-called tragedy.

Sister   Your brother will take good care of you, my little skylark. How could anyone love you as much as he does – a man who's always loved you more than he's loved anyone? A man who's all the men you'll ever need.

Girl   I don't want to be loved.

Sister   How can you say that? It's the only thing in this life that matters.

Girl   How dare you? You've never even had a man. You've never even *been* loved. You've spent your whole life totally unhappy and totally alone.

Sister   I've never been unhappy except out of sympathy for you.

Girl   Oh yes you have been unhappy: all those times I've caught you crying behind the curtains.

Sister   I cry regularly for no particular reason – just to build up credit – and now I've built up all that credit you'll never see me cry again. Why d'you want to leave?

Girl   To find him again.

Sister   You'll never find him again.

Girl   I know I'll find him again.

Sister   Rubbish. You know perfectly well your brother's been trying to for days and nights on end. To avenge you.

Girl   But I don't want to be 'avenged'. That's why I'll find him.

Sister   And what will you do when you do find him?

Girl   Tell him something.

Sister   What?

Girl   Something.

Sister   And where d'you think he is?

Girl   Little Chicago.

Sister   Why does my innocent dove want to throw herself away? Please, don't leave me. Don't leave me alone here. Not with your brother and your parents. Not alone in this house. Life without you won't be worth living and living will be meaningless. Don't leave me. I'm begging you not to leave me. I hate your brother and your parents and this house. You're all I've got to love, my innocent innocent child, and all I've got to live for.

Their **Father** *enters in a rage.*

Father   Your mother's hidden the beer. I'll knock her fucking senseless like the good old days. Why did I ever stop? True it wore me out, but I should've made myself, disciplined myself, or had the job done professionally. I should've kept it up like the good old days – regular beatings round the clock. But now look – turn a blind eye and the next thing you know she's hidden the beer, you conniving little bitches. (*He looks under the table.*) I had five bottles left and if they don't turn up I'll hit you five times each.

He goes.

Sister   My turtledove in Little Chicago! You must be – and you will be – so unhappy!

Their **Mother** *enters.*

Mother   Your father's drunk again. The cretin knocks back the beer, bottle after bottle, and what do the pair of

you do? Just stand there. Just stand there and leave it up
to me. You just stand there and watch him ruin us with
his drinking. You're a pair of little idiots with your
chatter chatter chatter. All you care about is your own
stupid little problems while I'm left to deal with that piss-
artist. What're you doing with that bag?

Sister   She's going to spend the night at a friend's.

Mother   At a friend's, at a friend's? What friend? What
are you girls up to? Why does she need to spend the night
at a friend's? Aren't the beds here good enough? Aren't
the nights here dark enough? If you were younger and I
was stronger I'd crack your heads together.

She goes.

Sister   I don't want you to be unhappy.

Girl   But I'm happy to be unhappy. Yes, there was a lot
of pain, but the pain's what I enjoyed.

Sister   I'll die if you leave me.

The **Girl** *picks up the bag and goes.*

Scene 8: Just before dying

Outside a late-night bar. Phone-booth.
With a great crash of broken glass, **Zucco** *comes flying
through the window.*
*Screams from within. A crowd of onlookers appears at the
doorway.*

Zucco
   'And thus was I created like the statue
   Of an athlete standing on a holy
   Pedestal, perfected by the fury
   Of the tempestuous sea raging vainly
   At my feet. Strong and naked, my brow thrust ...'

Prostitute   He'll catch his death. It's fucking freezing
out here.

Man   Don't you worry about him. He's sweating. He's plenty warm enough inside.

Zucco
   '. . . Into the abyss; hail and foam-enveloped;
   Buffeted by the storm-wracked nights, I raise
   These arms towards th' ethereal darkness.'

Man   Pissed out of his head.

Man   Rubbish. He's not been drinking.

Prostitute   He's just crazy. Why can't you leave him alone?

Bruiser   Leave him alone? He spends hours spouting that shit and you say leave him alone? One more time and I crack his skull open.

Prostitute (*goes to help* **Zucco** *up*)   No more fighting. Come on. No more fighting. You've already messed up that beautiful face of yours. Don't you want the girls to look at you any more? Faces are precious, lover-boy. You think a face is for life, then it's rearranged by some ugly bastard with no face to lose. But you've got so *much* to lose, lover-boy. Your face is like your balls – lose it and your whole life's fucked. You don't care now, but believe me, you will in the morning. Don't look at me like that or I'll start to cry. You're the kind of man who can make people cry just by looking at them.

Zucco *goes up to* **Bruiser** *and punches him.*

Prostitute   They're not going to start again, are they?

Bruiser   Don't tempt me, lover-boy, just don't tempt me.

Zucco *punches him again.* **Bruiser** *hits back. They fight.*

Prostitute   I'm calling the police. He's going to kill him.

Man   You're not calling anyone.

Man   And anyway, he's out for the count.

Zucco *gets up and follows* **Bruiser** *as he moves away. He clings on to him and punches him in the face.*

Prostitute   Ignore him. Leave him alone. He can hardly stand up.

Zucco   You gutless bollockless bastard. Come on. Fight.

Bruiser *sends him flying.*

Bruiser   He tries that again and I squash him like a fly.

Again **Zucco** *gets up and tries to make him fight.*

Prostitute (*to* **Bruiser**)   Don't hurt him, don't hurt him, you'll cripple him.

Bruiser *knocks* **Zucco** *out.*

Man   Well that takes care of that.

Prostitute   He's right, you've got no guts. It wasn't a fair fight.

Bruiser   A man doesn't let the same dog bite twice.

They go back into the bar.

Zucco *gets up and goes to the phone-booth. He picks up the phone, dials, and waits.*

Zucco   Take me away. Take me away from here. It's too hot in this fuck of a city. Take me to snowy Africa. Take me there before I die. Because nobody cares about anyone. The men need women and the women need men – but as for love, there *is* none. I get a hard-on with women out of sheer pity. I'd like to come back as a dog, and find a little happiness. A stray dog no one would notice, poking round the bins. I'd like to be the kind of yellow scab-infested stray people automatically avoid, poking round the bins till the end of time. What use are words when there's nothing to be said? They should stop teaching words. They should close the schools and enlarge the cemeteries. One year or a hundred – what difference does it make? Sooner or later we all of us have to die. And that's what makes the birds sing, and that's what makes them laugh at us.

Prostitute (*in the doorway*)   I told you he was crazy. That phone doesn't even work.

Zucco *drops the phone and sits back against the booth.* **Bruiser** *comes over.*

Bruiser   What's on your mind, lover-boy?

Zucco   I'm contemplating the immortality of the crab, the slug, and the dung-beetle.

Bruiser   Listen, my friend, I don't enjoy fighting. But there are limits to what a man can take, limits to how far he can be pushed. Why push me so far, eh? You want to die, or what?

Zucco   I don't *want* to die: I'm *going* to die.

Bruiser   Like everyone else, my friend.

Zucco   That's not a reason.

Bruiser   Maybe not.

Zucco   The trouble with beer is you think you're buying it but you're only renting it. I need a piss.

Bruiser   Go on then – before it's too late.

Zucco   Is it true that even the dogs despise me?

Bruiser   Dogs don't despise anyone. Dogs are the only creatures you can trust. Love you or hate you, they never judge you. And when everyone's washed their hands of you, there'll still be some dog somewhere waiting to lick the soles of your feet.

Zucco
  'Morte villana, di pietà nemica,
  di dolor madre antica,
  giudicio incontastabile gravoso,
  di te blasmar la lingua s'affatica.'

Bruiser   What about that piss?

Zucco Too late.

Dawn breaks.
Zucco *falls asleep.*

Scene 9: Delilah

A police station. A **Sergeant** *and a* **Superintendent.**
The **Girl** *enters, followed by her* **Brother,** *who remains by the door.*
The **Girl** *goes up to* **Zucco's** *picture and points to it.*

Girl I know him.

Super Know him? Really?

Girl Yes. Really. Extremely well.

Sergeant Who is he then?

Girl A secret agent. A friend.

Sergeant What about that character over there?

Girl My brother. He's come with me. I recognised that photo in the street and he said to come.

Sergeant You realise he's wanted by the police?

Girl Yes. I want him too.

Sergeant And this is a friend of yours?

Girl A friend – *yes.*

Sergeant The murderer of a policeman. You'll be arrested and charged with conspiracy, failure to report a crime and unlawful possession of a firearm.

Girl But my brother said to come and tell you. I'm not in unlawful possession of anything. I know him, that's all.

Sergeant Tell your brother he can go.

Super Are you deaf? Get out.

The **Brother** *leaves.*

Sergeant   What can you tell us about him?

Girl   Everything.

Sergeant   Is he a foreigner?

Girl   He's got a really faint but really really nice – yes – accent.

Super   Germanic?

Girl   I don't know what 'Germanic' means.

Sergeant   So ... he *told* you he was a secret agent. That's strange. Secret agents don't as a rule reveal the fact.

Girl   I told him I'd keep it a secret whatever happened.

Super   Congratulations. If everyone kept secrets like that our workload would be considerably lightened.

Girl   He told me he went on missions to Africa – in the mountains – where it snows all the time.

Sergeant   A German agent in Kenya.

Super   So our theories weren't so far off the mark after all.

Sergeant   Accurate in the extreme, Superintendent. (*To* **Girl**.) What about his name? D'you know it? You must if he's your friend.

Girl   Of course I do.

Super   Tell us.

Girl   Of course I know his name.

Super   Don't make fun of the police, young lady – unless you'd like a few bruises to take home.

Girl   I don't want any bruises. I know his name, but I just can't say it.

Sergeant   What d'you mean: you just can't say it?

Girl   I can feel it on my lips.

Super   On your lips? Feel it on your lips? How'd you like to be slapped and punched and have your hair pulled out, eh? You realise we have rooms here designed for just that purpose.

Girl   No. Please. It's there. It will come.

Sergeant   How about his first name? You must remember *that*. You must've slobbered it in his ear often enough.

Super   Come on – first name – anything – or it's off to the torture chamber.

Girl   Andreas.

Sergeant (*to* **Super**)   Andreas. *Very* interesting. (*To* **Girl**.) Are you sure?

Girl   No.

Super   I'm going to kill her.

Sergeant   Out with the bastard's name or you get a knuckle-fucking-sandwich. Hurry up. I'm warning you.

Girl   Angelo.

Sergeant   Spanish.

Super   Or Italian, or Brazilian, or Portuguese, or Mexican. I've even come across a Berliner called Julio.

Sergeant   Your experience, Superintendent, knows no bounds. (*To* **Girl**.) I'm losing my patience.

Girl   I know it's on the tip of my tongue.

Super   Shall we pull it out for you and have a look?

Girl   Angelo. Angelo ... Sugo or something like that.

Sergeant   Sugo? Like sugar?

Girl   Yes, like sugar. He told me his name was like a foreign word for sweet or sugary. (*She begins to cry.*) He was so sweet and kind.

Sergeant   I suppose there must be lots of foreign words for sweet and sugary.

Super   *Azucarado, zuccherato, sucrè, gezuckert, ocukrzony.*

Sergeant   Yes yes, I think we know all that.

Girl   Zucco. Zucco. Roberto Zucco.

Sergeant   Are you positive?

Girl   Yes. Positive.

Super   Zucco. With a Z?

Girl   With a Z, yes. Roberto with a Z.

Sergeant   Take her to make a statement.

Girl   What about my brother?

Super   Brother? What brother? Who needs a brother when you've got us?

They all go out.

Scene 10: The hostage

A park in broad daylight.
*An elegant **Lady** sitting on a bench.*
*Enter **Zucco**.*

Lady   Sit here beside me. Talk to me. I'm bored – let's have a conversation. I hate parks. Don't be shy. Do I intimidate you?

Zucco   I'm not shy.

Lady   But your hands are shaking like a boy about to have his first taste of sex. You have a nice face. You're a good-looking boy. Do you like women? You're almost too good-looking to like women.

Zucco   I do like women. I like them a lot.

Lady I suppose you mean these fresh-faced eighteen-year-olds.

Zucco I like all women.

Lady That's excellent news. And have you been brutal yet with a woman?

Zucco Never.

Lady Not even felt the desire? Surely you've at least felt the desire to treat one violently? It's a desire all men have had at some point without exception.

Zucco Not me. I'm gentle and peace-loving.

Lady You're a strange sort of person.

Zucco Did you come in a taxi?

Lady Certainly not. I can't bear taxi-drivers.

Zucco So you came in a car.

Lady Obviously. I didn't walk here – I live on the other side of town.

Zucco What kind of car is it?

Lady What – did you think it was a Porsche? No, it's a pathetic little car. My husband's a tight bastard.

Zucco What make?

Lady Mercedes.

Zucco Which model?

Lady 280 SE.

Zucco That's not pathetic.

Lady Maybe not – but he's a bastard all the same.

Zucco Who the hell's that? He keeps looking at you.

Lady That's my son.

Zucco Your son? Isn't he rather big?

Lady Not a day over fourteen. I'm not geriatric, you know.

Zucco   He looks older than that. Does he do sport?

Lady   That's *all* he does. Not only do I pay for him to belong to every club in town – tennis, hockey, golf – but then he expects me to drive him round to training sessions. He's a little prick, actually.

Zucco   He looks strong for his age. Give me the car-keys.

Lady   Of course. My pleasure. I suppose you want the car as well.

Zucco   Yes. The car as well.

Lady   Take it.

Zucco   Give me the keys.

Lady   Oh don't be so boring.

Zucco   Give me the keys.

He gets out the gun and puts it on his lap.

Lady   You must be mad. You don't play with a thing like that.

Zucco   Call your son.

Lady   Certainly not.

Zucco   (*threatens her with the gun*)   I said: call your son.

Lady   You must be out of your mind. (*Shouts to her son.*) Run for it. Back to the house. Just get the hell out.

As her son approaches, the **Lady** *gets up.* **Zucco** *holds the gun to her throat.*

Lady   Shoot me then, you idiot. I won't give you the keys – if only so you don't take me for a fool. My husband takes me for a fool, my son takes me for a fool, the maid takes me for a fool, so go on – shoot – it'll be one less fool. But you're not getting the keys. And it's your loss, because it's a superb car – leather seats, and dashboard in figured walnut. The loss will be entirely yours. So just stop making a scene. Look – those idiots are going to come over and start making comments. They'll call the police. Just look at the way they're licking their lips. It's their lucky day. I can't bear those people and their bloody comments. Go on: shoot. That way I won't have to hear them.

Zucco (*to the* **Child** – *her son*)   Keep back.

Man   Look at the way he's shaking.

Zucco   For christsake keep back. On the ground. Lie down.

Woman   It's the child making him afraid.

Zucco   Now – hands by your sides. Come closer. Crawl.

Woman   How's he supposed to crawl with his hands by his sides?

Man   It's not impossible. *I* could do it.

Zucco   Slowly. Hands behind your back. Keep your head down. Stop. (*The* **Child** *makes a movement.*) One false move and your mother dies.

Man   He's not joking either.

Man   Absolutely. He's serious. Poor kid.

Zucco   Promise you won't move?

Child   Promise.

Zucco   Keep your head right down on the ground. Now turn it slowly to the other side. Turn your head. I don't want you looking at us.

Child   But why are you afraid of me? What can I do? I'm a child. I don't want my mother to die. There's no need for you to be afraid – you're much stronger than me.

Zucco   Much stronger. Yes.

Child   So why are you afraid of me? What harm could I do you? I'm just a child.

Zucco   Not such a child as all that – and I'm not afraid.

Child   Yes you are. You're shaking. I can hear it in your voice.

Man   Here come the police.

Woman   Now he'll have something to shake about.

Man   More like laugh about.

Zucco (*to* **Child**)   Shut your eyes.

Child   They *are* shut, they *are* shut. *Christ* you're a scaredy-cat.

Zucco   Shut your mouth too.

Child   I'll shut whatever you like – but you're still a scaredy-cat – frightening a woman – pointing that stupid gun at her.

Zucco   Your mother's car – what kind is it?

Child   What d'you reckon? A Porsche?

Zucco   Shut up. Shut your face. Shut your mouth. Shut your eyes. Play dead.

Child   I don't know how to play dead.

Zucco   You'll soon find out. I'll kill your mother – then you'll see what playing dead means.

Woman   Poor kid.

Child   I'm playing dead, I'm playing dead.

Man   The police are keeping their distance.

Woman   Shit-scared, that's why.

Man   Not at all. It's strategy. They know what they're doing. Police techniques may not be obvious to the layman – but they know what they're doing, believe you me. He's basically had it.

Man   The woman too, if you ask me.

Man   Well you can't make an omelette without breaking the eggs.

Woman Just don't let him hurt the child – please God, not the child.

*Forcing the **Lady** forwards with the gun to her neck, **Zucco** goes up to the **Child** and puts one foot on his head.*

Woman Dear me, it's not easy being a child nowadays.

Man It wasn't any easier when *we* were kids.

Woman And I suppose *you* were attacked by a psychopath, were you?

Man I'm talking about the war actually – or have you forgotten?

Woman Oh really? I suppose the Germans trod on *your* face and attacked *your* mother, did they?

Man Worse than that actually, if you really want to know.

Woman Well it didn't stop you getting old and fat and living to tell the tale, did it?

Man There's no need to be offensive.

Woman My only concern is for the child – just for the child.

Man For godsake stop going on about that child. The woman's the one with a gun to her throat.

Woman Yes, but the child's the one who'll suffer.

Woman By the way, is that what you meant by special police techniques? Because you must be joking. They're miles away. They're shitting themselves.

Man The word I actually used was strategy.

Man Strategy my arse.

Police (*from a distance*) Drop your gun.

Woman Fantastic.

Woman Police to the rescue.

Man Some strategy.

Man   You'll see – when they go in for the kill.

Woman   There's only one person I can see going in for the kill round here.

Man   In fact it's practically a *fait accompli*.

Woman   That poor poor child.

Man   Excuse me, but if you go on any longer about that poor poor child, I'll slap you round the face.

Man   D'you think this is really the moment to be arguing? Dignity – *please*. We're witnessing a human tragedy. We're staring into the face of death.

Police (*from a distance*)   This is the police. Drop your gun. You are surrounded.

The onlookers burst out laughing.

Zucco   Tell her to give me the car-keys. It's a Porsche.

Lady   Idiot.

Woman   Give him the keys, give him the keys.

Lady   Absolutely not. He can get them himself.

Man   You're going to get your face blown right off, my darling.

Lady   So what? At least I'll be spared the sight of *your* ugly faces.

Woman   What an appalling woman.

Man   Nasty piece of work. There are so many cruel and unpleasant people in this world.

Woman   *Make* her hand them over. Surely one of you men can go through her pockets and find the keys?

Woman   What about you? If you suffered so much as a child. If the Germans stepped on your face and threatened your mother. Show us you've still got some balls – or one ball at least – even if it *is* small and shrivelled up.

Man With all respect, you deserve a slap round the face.
It's lucky for you I'm a gentleman.

Woman Go through her pockets – get the keys – *then*
slap me round the face.

*The **Man**, trembling, goes up, reaches out, feels in the*
***Lady**'s pocket, and takes out the keys.*

Lady Idiot.

Man (*triumphantly*) What about that then? What about
that? Get them to bring round the Porsche.

*The **Lady** laughs.*

Woman She's laughing. How can she laugh when her
child's about to die?

Woman How horrible.

Man She must be insane.

Man Give the keys to the police. They can at least deal
with that. Hopefully they at least know how to drive a car.

*The **Man** comes running back.*

Man It's not a Porsche, it's a Mercedes.

Man Which model?

Man 280 SE, I think. Beautiful machine.

Man Mercedes make a nice car.

Woman Whatever kind it is, just get it. Get it before he
kills us all.

Zucco I want a Porsche, not people taking the piss.

Woman Tell the police to find a Porsche. Don't argue
with him. He's mad, totally mad. Just find him a Porsche.

Man At least that's something they should be capable
of.

Man Don't count on it. They're still miles away.

Some of them head for the police.

Man   Look at us. We're just ordinary people and we've got more guts than they have.

Woman (*to the* **Child**)   You poor darling. Is that nasty foot hurting you?

Zucco   Shut up. No one talks to him. He's not to open his mouth. Come on – shut your eyes – don't move.

Man (*to the* **Lady**)   And may I ask how his mother's feeling?

Lady   Fine, thank you, absolutely fine. But I'd be feeling a great deal happier if you kept your big mouths shut and all went back to your fitted kitchens and screaming shitty little brats.

Woman   She's got no feelings, none at all.

Policeman (*from the other side of the crowd*)   Here are the car-keys. It's a Porsche. Over there. You can see it from here. (*To the crowd.*) Pass him the keys.

Man   *You* pass him the keys. Killers are your department.

Policeman   We have our reasons.

Woman   Reasons bullshit.

Man   I'm not touching those keys. It's not my job. I've got a wife and kids.

Zucco   I'll shoot the woman, then I'll put a bullet into my own head. I don't give a fuck about living. I don't give a fuck about anything, be*lieve* me. I've got six bullets. I'll kill five people – then I'll kill myself.

Woman   He means it, he means it. Let's get out of here.

Policeman   Don't move. You're making him anxious.

Man   You're the ones causing the anxiety by doing nothing.

Man   Just leave them to get on with it. There's a plan. There must be.

Policeman Don't move.

He puts the keys on the ground and uses a stick to push them to **Zucco** *through the legs of the crowd.* **Zucco** *slowly bends down, picks up the keys, and puts them in his pocket.*

Zucco The woman comes with me. Keep back.

Woman The child's safe. Thank goodness for that.

Man What about the woman though? What's going to happen to *her*?

Zucco I said: keep back.

Everyone backs away. Still holding the gun, **Zucco** *leans over, grabs the* **Child** *by the hair, and shoots him in the back of the neck. People scream and run. With the gun to the woman's throat,* **Zucco** *heads for the car across the almost deserted park.*

Scene 11: It's a deal

Reception of the Little Chicago hotel.
The **Madam** *in her armchair, the* **Girl** *waiting.*

Girl I'm ugly.

Madam Don't be such a silly baby.

Girl I'm fat. I've got a double chin and a double stomach to go with it – breasts like footballs – and it's a good thing I can't see my backside because I know for a fact that with every step I take it seesaws up and down behind me like two legs of bacon.

Madam You don't know what you're talking about.

Girl I *know* it does, I *know* it does. I know for a fact that dogs follow me in the street with their tongues hanging out dribbling slobber. Given half a chance they'd sink their teeth into me like meat on a slab.

Madam Whatever gave you that idea, you silly creature? You're pretty. You're well-rounded. And you've got a proper figure. D'you imagine a man appreciates some piece of dead twig he's frightened will snap off in his hands? Because what a man appreciates, my darling, is a nice round handful.

Girl   But I'd *like* to be thin. I'd *like* to be a piece of dead twig they were frightened of snapping.

Madam   Well *I* wouldn't. And besides just because you're fat today doesn't mean you won't be thin tomorrow. Women go through changes in their lives – it's not something to worry about. When I was a kid like you I was so thin you could almost see through to the other side of me – just a scrap of skin and a few bones. Not a breast in sight. As flat as a boy. Which made me pretty angry, since I wasn't too fond of boys in those days. I used to dream of a beautiful body and nice breasts. So I made myself some out of cardboard. But of course the boys found me out, and whenever they went past, they elbowed me in the chest and completely flattened them. But after a few goes, I fixed a needle inside – and believe me, they screamed to high bloody heaven. And after that – as you can see – I began to fill out and put on some flesh and I was a happy woman. So stop worrying, you little cuckoo: just because you're fat today doesn't mean you won't be thin tomorrow.

Girl   So what? I'm still fat, ugly and miserable.

The **Brother** *enters, talking to a* **Pimp**. *Neither pays any attention to the* **Girl**.

Pimp (*impatiently*)   That's too much.

Brother   You can't *put* a price on it.

Pimp   Everything has a price – and yours is far too high.

Brother   But if you can put a price on something you're saying it can't be worth much. You're saying we can haggle, that the price can go up and down. Whereas what I've done is set an abstract price for something priceless. It's like a Picasso – have you ever seen someone say a

Picasso's too expensive? Have you ever seen the owner
drop the price of a Picasso? Because in situations like that
the price is an abstraction.

Pimp   It may be an abstraction, but it's still one that
goes from my pocket into yours. And I suppose the hole it
makes in my pocket is an abstraction too?

Brother   A hole like that soon fills up. Believe me,
you'll fill it up so fast you'll forget the price you paid in
less time than the time you're taking to discuss it. Not
that there's anything here to discuss. Make the best deal
of the year or remain a poor man. Take it or leave it.

Pimp   Calm down, calm down – I'm thinking.

Brother   That's fine – you think – but don't take too
much time or I'll have to take my sister back to her
mother.

Pimp   OK. It's a deal.

Brother (*to* **Girl**)   Hey – pussycat – it's time you
thought about powdering that shiny nose of yours.

They watch her go out.

So ... My Picasso?

Pimp   I still say it's expensive.

Brother   She'll make you so much money you won't
even remember what you paid.

Money changes hands.

Pimp   When can you make her available?

Brother   Calm down, calm down – there's plenty of
time.

Pimp   No there is not 'plenty of time'. You've got the
money, I want the girl.

Brother   You've *got* the girl – to all intents and
purposes.

Pimp   Now you've got the money you're regretting it.

Brother   I regret nothing, nothing at all. I'm thinking.

Pimp   Thinking about what? This isn't the moment. I want to know when.

Brother   Tomorrow, the day after tomorrow.

Pimp   Why not today?

Brother   OK – why not today – why not tonight?

Pimp   Why not right now?

Brother   Just ease up, will you.

They hear the **Girl**'s *footsteps.*

Brother   Right now. OK, it's a deal.

The **Brother** *rushes off and hides in one of the rooms. The* **Girl** *enters.*

Girl   Where's my brother?

Pimp   He's asked me to take care of you.

Girl   I want to know where my brother is.

Pimp   Listen, you're coming with me.

Girl   I don't want to go with you.

Madam   Just do exactly what you're told, you little fat fool. A brother's orders are final.

The **Girl** *goes out with the* **Pimp**. *The* **Brother** *emerges from the room and sits opposite the* **Madam**.

Brother   It wasn't my idea – I swear to you it wasn't. But she went on and on, on and on about coming here and going on the game. She's looking for someone – don't ask me who – but someone she has to find. And this is where she thinks she'll find him. It was not my idea. No older brother ever watched over a sister the way I have. No one was ever loved the way I've loved my poor poor darling sister. There's nothing I can do. We're just victims of evil. It was her idea – all I did was give in to her. I've never been able to say no to my baby sister. We're just victims of evil and there's no escape from it. (*He cries.*)

Madam   You piece of shit.

Scene 12: Railway station

Zucco *and the* **Lady**.

Zucco   Roberto Zucco.

Lady   Why d'you keep saying your name all the time?

Zucco   I'm frightened I'll forget it.

Lady   People don't forget their names. Your name must be the last thing you forget.

Zucco   Not me. I keep forgetting it. I can see it written inside my head, but less and less well, less and less clearly, as if it's fading. I have to peer closer and closer before I can read it. I'm frightened of ending up not knowing my name.

Lady   I won't forget it. I'll be your memory.

Zucco (*after a pause*)   I like women. I like them too much.

Lady   You can never like them too much.

Zucco   There aren't any women I don't like. I can't get enough of them.

Lady   In which case you like me.

Zucco   Of course I do. You're a woman.

Lady   Why have you brought me here?

Zucco   Because I'm going to catch a train.

Lady   What about the Porsche? Why don't you go off in the Porsche?

Zucco   I don't want to be noticed. A train is anonymous.

Lady   And am I supposed to come with you?

Zucco No.

Lady Why not? There's no reason for me not to come. From the moment I set eyes on you the impression has not been unfavourable. I'm coming with you. And besides, that's what you want – or you'd have killed me by now or let me go.

Zucco I need you to give me money for the train. I don't have any. My mother was supposed to give me some but she forgot.

Lady They always do. Where are you going to go?

Zucco Venice.

Lady Venice? What a peculiar idea.

Zucco D'you know Venice?

Lady Naturally. Everyone knows Venice.

Zucco It's where I was born.

Lady Brilliant. I always thought no one was born in Venice, but everyone died there. The babies must be born covered in dust and spiders' webs. At any rate, France has certainly cleaned you up. I can't see one speck of dust. This country must be a wonderful detergent. Brilliant.

Zucco I have to get away. I absolutely have to. I won't be caught. I won't be locked away. All these people are scaring the shit out of me.

Lady Scaring the shit? Be a man, can't you. You've got a gun – they'd run a mile if you just took it out of your pocket.

Zucco I'm shit-scared *because* I'm a man.

Lady Well *I'm* not scared. After everything you've made me go through I'm still not scared – and never have been.

Zucco That's because you're not a man.

Lady You're much too complicated.

Zucco If they catch me, they'll lock me away. And if they lock me away, I'll go insane. I'm *already* going insane. Police everywhere. People everywhere. It's like being locked away already. Stop looking at them. Stop it.

Lady Do I really look like I'm going to give you away? Idiot. I could've done that a long time ago. This scum disgusts me. Your company is infinitely more pleasant.

Zucco Just look at them all: all mad and full of hatred. *They're* the killers. I've never seen so many killers all at once. One flick of the switch and they'd start murdering each other. I don't understand why the switch doesn't flick right now – inside their brains. Because they're all primed to kill. Like laboratory rats. Like rats in a cage. They want to kill. You can see it in their eyes – in the way they walk – the way their fists are clenched in their pockets. I can spot a killer at a glance – their clothes are thick with blood. This place is full of them. We have to stay calm and not move. We have to avoid their eyes. They mustn't see us – we have to be transparent. Or otherwise – if we *do* look into their eyes, and they catch us looking, if they start to look back at us and stare, the switch in their heads will flick on and they'll kill and they'll kill. If just one of them starts, everyone here will murder everyone else. One flick of the switch is all it takes.

Lady Shut up. You're being hysterical. I'll go and get the tickets. Just calm down or you're going to give us away. (*After a pause.*) Why did you kill him?

Zucco Kill who?

Lady My son, you idiot.

Zucco Because he was a little prick.

Lady Who told you that?

Zucco You did. You told me he was a little prick. You told me he took you for a fool.

Lady And what if I *liked* being taken for a fool? What if

I *liked* little pricks? What if I liked little pricks more than anything in the world – more than all the big bastards? What if little pricks were the only thing I *didn't* detest?

Zucco Then you should've told me.

Lady I *did* tell you, you idiot.

Zucco Then you shouldn't've refused me the keys. You shouldn't've humiliated me. I didn't want to kill him, but after that business with the Porsche one thing simply led to another.

Lady Liar. Nothing 'led' to anything – everything went wrong. *I* had the gun pointing at me, so why was *he* the one who had his head blown apart with blood everywhere?

Zucco If it'd been your head, there would've been blood everywhere too.

Lady But I wouldn't've had to see it – *would* I – idiot. I don't give a damn about *my* blood – it's not my affair. But his blood *was* my affair. Because I'm the one who damn well pumped it into his veins. It was *my affair*. And my affairs are not something you splatter about in front of a bunch of idiots in a park. Now I've nothing left to call my own. Anyone could be stepping in the only thing that was really mine. And in the morning the gardeners will wash it away. What's left for me now – well? What's left for me now?

Zucco *stands*.

Zucco I'm going.

Lady I'm coming with you.

Zucco Stay where you are.

Lady You don't even have the money for the train. You haven't even given me time to let you have it. You don't give anyone time to help you. You're like a flick-knife – open one moment – snapped shut and pocketed the next.

Zucco I don't need help.

Lady Everyone needs help.

Zucco Don't start crying. You've got that look of a woman who's going to start crying. I hate that.

Lady You told me you liked women. All of them. Even me.

Zucco Not when they get that look as if they're going to start crying.

Lady I promise you I won't.

She starts to cry. **Zucco** *moves away.*

Lady What about your name, you idiot? You're probably already incapable of saying it. Who'll remember it for you? You've forgotten it already, I know you have. I'm the only one who remembers it now. I'm your memory and you're leaving without me.

Zucco *goes. The* **Lady** *remains seated, watching the trains.*

Scene 13: Ophelia

The same place. Night.
The station is deserted. The sound of rain.
The **Sister** *enters.*

Sister Where's my innocent dove? What filth have they dragged her through? What vile cage have they locked her in? What twisted lecherous animals are stalking round her? I have to find you, my turtledove, and I'll keep on looking until it kills me.

Pause.

Of all the disgusting animals on this earth the most disgusting is the human male. That smell they have revolts me. The smell of sewer rats, or pigs in muck. The stagnant smell of rotting corpses.

Pause.

The male is filthy. Men don't wash. They treat the filth

and revolting substances they secrete like some precious and untouchable resource, storing it on their bodies. Men can't smell each other because all men smell the same. That's why they go round together all the time – and why they visit prostitutes – because only prostitutes can tolerate the smell – for money. I washed that little child so many times. Bathed her before dinner, bathed her in the mornings. Scrubbed her back and scrubbed her hands. Scrubbed under her nails. Washed her hair every day. Cut her nails. Washed her whole body every day with warm water and soap. I kept her white as a dove and preened her feathers like a turtledove. I protected her and kept her safe in a clean cage so as not to have her spotless whiteness spattered by the filth of this world, by the filthiness of men. So she would not be tainted by the tainted smell of men. And the rat of rats – the stinking pig, the degenerate male who sullied her, who dragged her through the mud and pulled her by the hair to his heap of dung – was her own brother. I should've killed him. I should've poisoned him. I should've stopped him stalking round my turtledove's cage. I should've wrapped barbed wire round my true love's cage. I should've stamped the rat dead and burned him in the stove.

Pause.

Everything here is filthy. This whole city is filthy and teeming with men. Let the rain fall and let it keep on falling. Let it fall on that heap of dung and softly wash my little turtledove.

Scene 14: The arrest

Little Chicago.
Two **Police officers.**
Prostitutes – and among them, the **Girl.**

1st Officer   Seen anyone?

2nd Officer   It's ridiculous. This job is ridiculous.

Stuck here like a couple of bollards. We might just as well
be back on traffic duty.

1st Officer   It's not ridiculous. This is where he killed
the sergeant.

2nd Officer   Exactly: the one place he'll never come
back to.

1st Officer   The murderer always returns to the scene
of the crime.

2nd Officer   Come back here? What makes you think
he'd do that? He didn't leave anything behind – not even a
suitcase. He's not crazy. We're just a couple of bollards
with no *raison d'être*.

1st Officer   He'll be back.

2nd Officer   Instead of this we could be having drinks
on the house, chatting to the girls or taking a little stroll
somewhere with all these other quiet law-abiding citizens.
Little Chicago must be the most law-abiding place in
town.

1st Officer   But where there's ash, there's fire.

2nd Officer   Fire? What fire exactly are you talking
about? Even the young ladies here are as quiet and law-
abiding as check-out girls. Their clients stroll around as if
it's a park. And the pimps do their tours of inspection like
bookshop assistants checking the shelves to see that
nothing's been stolen. So what d'you mean: fire? I'm
prepared to bet our friend won't be back – or the drinks
are on me.

1st Officer   Well he definitely went back home after
killing his father.

2nd Officer   Because he had stuff to do.

1st Officer   What stuff to do?

2nd Officer   Killing his mother. But once he'd done
that, he never went back. And because he's got no more
sergeants left to kill, he won't be back here either. I feel

like an idiot. I can feel my arms and legs growing leaves and roots. I can feel myself merging into the concrete. Come on: let's slip inside for a drink while it's still quiet – while everyone's taking their quiet little stroll. I mean can you really see anyone who looks like a killer?

1st Officer   Killers never do look like killers. Killers go for quiet little strolls in the crowd just like you and me.

2nd Officer   Then he must be mad.

1st Officer   A killer is mad by definition.

2nd Officer   Not necessarily. Even *I* can think of times when I've felt like killing somebody.

1st Officer   Exactly – those are the times you nearly went mad.

2nd Officer   Could well be, could well be.

1st Officer   No question.

Zucco *enters.*

2nd Officer   But the fact is – even if I *was* mad – even if I *was* a killer – you still wouldn't catch me strolling about at the scene of the crime.

1st Officer   Who the hell's that?

2nd Officer   Who's what?

1st Officer   Over there. Taking a quiet little stroll.

2nd Officer   Everyone here's taking a quiet little stroll. Little Chicago's turning into a kind of children's playground.

1st Officer   The one in the army fatigues.

2nd Officer   Yes, I can see.

1st Officer   Remind you of anyone?

2nd Officer   Possibly, possibly.

1st Officer   Might almost be *him*.

2nd Officer   Don't be absurd.

Girl (*sees* **Zucco**)   Roberto!

She throws her arms round him and kisses him.

1st Officer   It is him.

2nd Officer   Absolutely no doubt about it.

Girl   I've looked and looked for you, Roberto – and I've
betrayed you. I've cried so much I've turned into a tiny
island in the middle of a sea of tears, and now the last
waves are drowning me. I've suffered so much my
suffering could fill up the earth's chasms and flood out
from its volcanoes. I want to stay with you, Roberto. I
want to watch over your every heartbeat and your every
breath. I want to press my ear against you and hear the
workings of your body, tending to your body like a
mechanic tending a machine. I'll keep all your secrets –
I'll be your suitcase full of secrets – I'll be the bag where
you store away your mysteries. I'll look after your
weapons, and protect them from rust. You'll be my agent
and my secret.
And I'll be the suitcase you travel with
and the one who carries it
and the one who loves you.

1st Officer (*going up to* **Zucco**)   Identify yourself.

Zucco   I'm the murderer of my father, my mother, a
police sergeant, and a child. I'm a killer.

The **Officers** *take him away.*

Scene 15: Zucco in the sun

The prison rooftops, noon.
Throughout the scene no one is visible, except **Zucco** *when he
climbs to the top of the roof.*
We hear the mingled voices of prisoners and prison officers.

Voice   Roberto Zucco has escaped.

Voice   Again.

Voice   Who was guarding him?

Voice   Who was responsible?

Voice   We must look like fucking idiots.

Voice   You *do* look like fucking idiots.

Laughter.

Voice   No talking!

Voice   He must have accomplices.

Voice   He *doesn't* have accomplices. That's why he always manages to get away.

Voice   On his own.

Voice   Totally alone – like a hero.

Voice   The corridors need to be thoroughly searched.

Voice   He's lying low somewhere.

Voice   He's curled up sweating in some little hole.

Voice   He won't be sweating because of *you* lot.

Voice   He won't be sweating at all – he'll be laughing in your fucking faces.

Voice   He's laughing in everyone's fucking face.

Voice   He won't get far.

Voice   This is a modern prison. Escape's not an option.

Voice   It's impossible.

Voice   Physically impossible.

Voice   Zucco's had it.

Voice   He may've had it – but in the meantime he's climbing the roof and laughing in your fucking faces.

Zucco, *barefoot and bare-chested, reaches the top of the roof.*

Voice   What are you doing up there?

Voice   Come down immediately.

Laughter.

Voice   You've had it this time, Zucco.

Laughter.

Voice   Hey – Zucco – tell us how you manage to never spend more than an hour in prison.

Voice   What's the secret?

Voice   Where did you slip out? What's the trick?

Zucco   Go upwards. Don't try and go over the walls, because beyond the walls are still more walls: prison goes on for ever. You can only escape from the rooftops, towards the sun. They'll never put a wall between the sun and the earth.

Voice   But what about the guards?

Zucco   If you can't see the guards, they don't exist. And anyway, I could hold five of them in one hand and crush them in one go.

Voice   Where does it come from, Zucco? Where d'you get your strength?

Zucco   By charging, not walking. By not seeing the obstacles. And not seeing them means they collapse of their own accord. I'm strong and alone. I'm a rhino.

Voice   But what about your mother and father? It's wrong to harm your parents.

Zucco   But normal to kill them.

Voice   But not to kill a child, Zucco – not a child. It's your *enemies* you kill – people who can defend themselves. Not a child.

Zucco   I don't have enemies and I never attack. If I crush other living creatures it's not because I'm evil but because I step on them without seeing them.

Voice   Have you got money – money stashed away somewhere?

Zucco   I've no money. Anywhere. I don't need money.

Voice   You're a hero, Zucco.

Voice   He's a Goliath.

Voice   He's a Samson.

Voice   Who's Samson?

Voice   A gangster from Marseilles.

Voice   I knew him in prison. A real animal. He could lay out ten men at a time.

Voice   Liar.

Voice   With his bare hands.

Voice   With the jawbone of an ass, actually. And he wasn't from Marseilles.

Voice   Some woman dropped him in the shit.

Voice   That's right. Delilah. The business with the hair.

Voice   You can always trust a woman to betray you.

Voice   If it wasn't for women we'd all be free.

The sun climbs higher, shining with extraordinary intensity. A great wind begins to blow.

Zucco   Look at the sun.

The courtyard becomes completely silent.

Can't you see anything? Can't you see how it moves from side to side?

Voice   We can't see a thing.

Voice   The sun's hurting our eyes. It's dazzling us.

Zucco   But look what's coming out of it. The sun has an erection. That's where the wind's coming from.

Voice   The sun has a *what*? An *erection*?

Voice   Shut your faces!

Zucco   Move your head – see how it moves as you do.

Voice   How *what* moves? *I* can't see anything moving.

Voice   How can anything up there be moving? It's all been nailed and bolted into place since the beginning of time.

Zucco   It's the source of the wind.

Voice   We can't see any more. There's too much light.

Zucco   Turn to the east and it turns there too. Turn to the west and it follows you.

A hurricane begins to blow. **Zucco** *sways.*

Voice   He's mad. He's going to fall.

Voice   Stop it, Zucco – you're going to get yourself killed.

Voice   He's crazy.

Voice   He's going to fall.

The sun rises higher, with the blinding brilliance of an atomic explosion. Nothing else can be seen.

Voice (*shouts out*)   He's falling!

Methuen Modern Plays

include work by

Methuen Student Editions

For a Complete Catalogue of Methuen Drama titles
write to:

Methuen Drama
Michelin House
81 Fulham Road
London SW3 6RB